I HATE CHRISTMAS

A Manifesto for the Modern-Day Scrooge

I HATE CHRISTMAS

A Manifesto for the Modern-Day Scrooge

DANIEL BLYTHE

First published in Great Britain in 2005 by
Allison & Busby Limited
Bon Marché Centre
241-251 Ferndale Road
London SW9 8BJ
http://www.allisonandbusby.com

A catalogue record for this book is available from
the British Library.

10 9 8 7 6 5 4 3

ISBN 0 7490 8216 X

Printed and bound in Great Britain by
Bookmarque Ltd, Croydon, Surrey

DANIEL BLYTHE was born in 1969 and educated at Maidstone Grammar School and St John's College, Oxford. After starting his writing career as an author of *Doctor Who* fiction, he went on to write the acclaimed novels *The Cut* and *Losing Faith*, as well as *The Encyclopaedia of Classic 80s Pop* and *Dadlands: The Alternative Handbook for New Fathers*. He is also a Creative Writing tutor and occasionally co-presents programmes for BBC Local Radio. Daniel is married and lives with his family on the edge of Sheffield, a stone's throw from the wild and windswept Peak District. In his spare time he likes to sleep, ponder the meaning of life and have a nice little sit down with a cup of tea.

Also by Daniel Blythe

Fiction

The Cut
Losing Faith

Non-Fiction

The Encyclopaedia of Classic 80s Pop
Dadlands: The Alternative Handbook for New Fathers

The Christmas List: with thanks

- A Chocolate Orange to the family (Rachel, Ellie and Sam) for leaving me alone in the attic.

- Trivial Pursuit to David Simms, for advice on curmudgeonly rantings.

- A novelty jumper to David Shelley for switching on the lights and some amusing socks to Susie and the team for keeping the fire stoked.

- A *Best Christmas Hits* CD to Caroline Montgomery, for tea and empathy.

- Some herbal infusions to Adam Curtis (and the chicks) for a fascinating excursion into natural history.

CONTENTS

'liiiiiiiit's Chriiiiiiiist-maaaaaas!'

Ah, the seasonal call of Sir Nodsworth Holder. Perhaps it makes your bosom swell with festive joy. Or maybe you just want to deck the overly badged, flamboyantly booted twit, knock off his unnecessary headgear and tell him to get back in his box.

When you hear Sir Cliff, Michael Bublé, Wizzard and Jona Lewie echoing through the tinselled aisles of Tesco, do you start panting for joy and immediately planning which shade of socks you are going to buy for Uncle Bert this year – or do you develop a twitch and immediately need to flee the country and head for the nearest holly-free zone?

What about the city illuminations? Do the coloured searchlights of Oxford Street fill you with wonder and awe as if you were a 6-year-old again – or do you find them rather sinister, as if they are designed to pick out unbelievers for people to throw snowballs at? Do you wish they'd spent the money on something more sensible?

Then there's the prospect of having the whole family packed into your front room for the day, trying to look pleased as they unpack yet another scarf, bottle of cheap perfume or box of Roses – before having the annual argument over the fifth repeat of the 1996 *Only Fools And Horses* special. Does the thought delight you? Or would you rather, like one of the wacky characters you'll read about in this book, escape into a nuclear bunker for the whole of the festive season?

When the first flakes of snow start to fall, maybe you feel a thrill and immediately have the urge to open the sherry and the Twiglets and put your valuable old 78 of Bing Crosby's 'White

Christmas' on the gramophone. Or perhaps you wonder how the hell you are going to de-ice the car and dig it out in the morning, and decide that you'd rather express your feelings by playing some Nirvana at full volume against the neighbours' walls.

Yes, they say, it seems to get earlier every year. So, dip into this cornucopia of antidotes to seasonal joy. See the dark side of the angels, the flipside of the chocolate coins, the carols, the festive bargains, and what Ronnie Barker in *Porridge* referred to as 'all that swaddling'. It's a book for all those whose gut reaction to the festive season is a large bag of Mr Scrooge's Special Bah Humbugs. A handbook for everyone who wishes that the bloody Snowman would drop the cute kid from a very large height to the accompaniment of 'Walking in the Air'.

It's for anyone whose heart sinks at the prospect of passing round the Quality Street and finding that only the horrible toffees are left. It's for you if, during the Queen's annual piece of patronising waffle, you've briefly considered turning to the cause of Republicanism (even if you were brought back to your senses with the single thought: 'President Blair'…).

It's somewhere to retreat to while the sprouts are steaming, while Gran's swigging the cheap Glen Campbell cooking whisky and a nearby 5-year-old is bashing the hell out of 'Hark The Herald Angels Sing' on the new electronic xylophone which Santa unwisely brought her.

If you feel like being a curmudgeon at Christmas, you are not alone. Don't feel guilty about it. A season of enforced joy is so dangerously close to a season of enforced misery that they may as well be the same thing.

And maybe, in sampling the following anthology of seasonal suffering, you'll draw some comfort from the fact that somewhere, a great many people are actually having a worse time than you.

Merry Christmas.

Yeah, right.

2

Joy to the World

Do You Hate Christmas? The Ultimate Quiz

1 **What is the most enjoyable thing about Christmas?**
a) It celebrates the birth of Our Lord Jesus Christ.
b) It gives people the chance to get out and indulge their otherwise repressed passion for consumer items they don't really need.
c) It brings families together in a spirit of love and unity.
d) It's all over by Boxing Day.

2 **What do you consider to be a suitable date for beginning to discuss 'what we are doing at Christmas this year'?**
a) 1st January.
b) 1st August.
c) Some time in December.
d) Who cares?

3 **What is a reasonable time of year to begin advertising Christmas hampers, food, television programmes, bargains, toys and God knows what else?**
a) Early October.
b) Early November.
c) Early December.
d) I don't wish to see any of it advertised.

4 **How would you most like to spend a free weekend in the middle of December?**

a) Making mince pies and mulled wine for the Women's Institute party.

b) Traipsing round endless over-lit shops filled with pale, zombie-like people weighing themselves down with bulging shopping bags.

c) With your feet up, reading the newspaper.

d) Doing anything unrelated to Christmas.

5 **What is the best way of dealing with overenthusiastic carol-singers?**

a) Paying them.

b) Asking them nicely to go away.

c) Cold water.

d) Machine-gun posts and boiling oil.

6 **What is your reaction when you see shop assistants dressed up in tinsel and Santa-hats?**

a) Great – really getting into the spirit of things.

b) Amused tolerance.

c) They look a bit silly but it's up to them.

d) What stupid plonkers.

7 **What would you like to be Christmas number one?**

a) Something traditional – 'Merry Christmas Everybody' by Slade, or Sir Cliff's latest one.

b) Novelty thing by a TV character, or a boy-band ballad.

c) Something completely different – say, a Norwegian electro-Goth anthem or a three-minute art-rock masterpiece totally unrelated to Christmas.

d) Go away. As if I care.

8 What happens when you hear the inevitable sleigh bells and ding-dong music heralding a BBC Christmas trailer?

a) You rejoice – that magical time has come again.
b) You look forward to some innovative quality television.
c) You remark that it gets earlier every year.
d) You reach for your revolver.

9 How likely are you to describe Christmas as 'the most magical time of year'?

a) Definitely will – I love it.
b) Maybe after a pint or two.
c) I probably wouldn't go that far.
d) You're just taking the piss now, aren't you?

10 What is the true meaning of Christmas?

a) Gathering families together in festive spirit for a joyous celebration.
b) The birth of Our Lord Jesus Christ.
c) Piling your trolley high with crates of booze, dates, nuts and chocolates.
d) A travesty – a once-noble celebration going back to pagan times, first hijacked by the Christians and now firmly in the hands of grasping profiteers.

If you scored...

Mostly (a): You are a fully paid-up, rose-tinted-spectacled, brainwashed Christmas-lover and so you will probably hate this book.

Mostly (b): Maybe through obligation rather than true love, you look forward to the festive season – but secretly harbour a desire to get away from it all.

Mostly (c): There's hope for you. You're a traditionalist at heart, but a streak of anarchy makes you want to get on the roof and shout, 'Santa doesn't exist!'

Mostly (d): You are a modern-day Scrooge and this book will teach you nothing, but you may want to read it to have your views validated.

A Christmas Story...
for people having a bad day

Father Christmas, never the happiest of souls (all that ho-ho-ho-ing is just good PR, and it's strictly business anyway) was mightily pissed off. Several of the elves had gone down with MRSA (picked up in a National Elf hospital) and the New Deal elves were having problems producing the toys as quickly as the regulars. By December the twenty-third, they were well behind schedule, and Santa was starting to feel the pressure.

At lunchtime on Christmas Eve, Mrs Claus happened to mention that her mum was coming, which just made Santa Claus even more stressed. And then when he went out to harness the reindeer, he found that three of them were drunk on his cheap rum and the rest had absconded somewhere.

Still, he could always start loading up the sleigh, so he did – until it cracked under the weight of all the PlayStations, Barbie houses and Xboxes. This never happened when all the little buggers wanted was an Enid Blyton paperback and an orange, fumed Santa Claus quietly, lighting a fag – which promptly set his beard on fire. Frantically thumping the sparks from what remained of his facial hair, Santa stomped off to the drinks cabinet to pour himself a large shot of whisky – only to find the New Deal elves had pinched it all and only the Shloer and the Sunny Delight was left.

It seemed things couldn't get any worse.

Just then the doorbell rang, and an irritable Santa stomped to the door. He opened it, and there was a smiling little angel carrying an enormous Christmas tree. The angel said, very cheerfully, 'Merry Christmas, Santa! Isn't it a lovely day? I've got a beautiful tree for you here. Where would you like me to stick it?'

And so began the tradition of the little angel on top of the Christmas tree.

Countdown Conundrum

At what point did Christmas become something for which it was acceptable to have a 'countdown'? You don't get it for Easter, or the spring bank holiday. Even those other 'occasions' which have been invented by a satanic cartel of Interflora, Clinton's Cards and Thornton's chocolates don't overdo it that much. You don't have huge, illuminated displays in the main streets of the identikit towns up and down the country, shouting out at you that there are 'Sixteen more shopping days left until Mothering Sunday!'

You are calmly going about your own business in WHSmith one Monday in mid-August and chuckling at the way they always get the 'Back To School' stationery displays up at least a week before anybody actually finishes the summer term. You may be dragging a small child around with you, wondering how much longer you can stop it from screaming with the promise of a chocolate bar and a go on the miserable Postman Pat car – and then you see it. The Christmas display. It starts small – just a few baubles and a bit of tinsel, perhaps, and a rack of cards. But it's there.

You laugh hollowly, wondering who on earth would be contemplating the supreme hell of Christmas when they still have the prospect of filling five more weeks of the endless, stuffy, sweaty, smelly and achingly sun-blasted days of the summer holidays, those weeks when the heat clamps you like a huge rubber glove and won't let go, and you have to mow the bloody lawn every week… (But let's leave that for another time.) No, you can't believe that anybody can seriously be planning so far ahead, be so obsessed by the prospect of that day in December that they actually want to see the trees and the lights go up. They can't possibly already want to start reading tips in the magazines about how to prepare the perfect mince pie, and learning about what Dale Winton, Michael Winner, Lisa from *Karaoke Idol* and the cast of *Hollyoaks* are all going to be doing for the festive season.

But they do. And you are made to feel like an old curmudgeon for moaning about it. 'Ooh, all these people who moan that Christmas gets earlier every year. They should just shut up and get on with enjoying it.' Well, actually, no. We shouldn't. It's about time we made a stand. *Why* do they have to start promoting it in August? It's not like we don't know it's coming. It's not as if we look at the 'Christmas Bargains Galore!' display of catalogues in the window of Boots and think, 'Ooh, thanks for that! Do you know, I wasn't sure if we'd be having Christmas this year. When is it again? December the what? Twenty-fifth? Oh, I might be able to make that. Let's have a little look in the diary. Hmm, do you know, I don't seem to be doing anything then for a few days. I'll pencil it in. Thanks for giving me decent notice.'

Can we not just take it for granted that people kind of know, actually, that Christmas is coming this year, just as it has every year for the last several hundred? How about lobbying your MP to have a new law made – one which imposes a blanket ban on even mentioning the bloody thing until mid-December? Even then, we'd have a good couple of weeks of build-up and promotion.

Worth a thought?

Deck the Halls
(and the porch, the roof, the garden path and the herbaceous border)

The art of Christmas decoration in suburbia has gone beyond simple jocular, festive activity. It is now a full-blown orgy of competition, possibly fuelled by a growing consumerism and aspiration across all social classes.

It seems to have grown exponentially through the years of Thatcherism and beyond. Who, in the 1970s, festooned their entire roof with flashing fairy lights or displayed a gigantic luminous reindeer on the porch? Nobody – for one thing, the government was keeping everyone on their toes by switching off the electricity every couple of days.

One particularly memorable power cut – I think it was in 1976 – actually happened on Christmas Eve itself. The question of how to power the lights on the tree was somewhat secondary to the challenge my mother would face in cooking an entire turkey with roast potatoes and vegetables for four people on a Campingaz® stove in the garden shed. Thankfully, it didn't come to that, but I still have a pathological fear of the smell of oil lamps and the sound of the *Nine Lessons and Carols* crackling from a battery radio.

You do wonder how anybody can get pleasure from having their entire house illuminated like the seafront at Blackpool. Perhaps it is a symptom of the growing insularity of the British nuclear family. In our day, children used to go into town to see the Christmas lights being switched on by Brother Beyond,

Limahl, or Philip Schofield and Gordon the Gopher. There was also the added thrill that some cowboy might have wired the switch up clumsily and that you could be in with a chance of seeing several thousand volts being jolted through, say, Glenn Medeiros. These days, though, they just put the whole lot on the roof, in the mistaken assumption that it costs less than a day at the seaside – and all without the bonus thrill of expecting the live incineration of D-list celebrities.

It's ironic that the British homeowner – having spent a decade becoming a creature of restraint, an acolyte at the magnolia-hued altar of Ann Maurice's house-doctrine – should, once a year, rediscover the joy of the garish. So what has happened? Is this a kind of 'bling-bling merrily on high' makeover? Or is it simply a huge joke, a way of inflicting your bad taste on the rest of the world while you sit inside in your low-lit, stripped-pine, minimalist comfort?

Let's hear from Jonathan Shaw, director of online lights supply firm Christmas Lights Direct. 'The American trend is coming over here,' says Jonathan, as if this were somehow a good thing. 'Over there, the whole street goes barmy at Christmas.' (Only at Christmas?) 'When we were children, very few people trimmed up outside – but now, more and more people are starting to put something in their garden.' Seemingly unaware of the comic effect he produces by using the chirpy expression 'trimmed up', Jonathan goes on to add that their most expensive line was a 12-foot sign saying *Merry Christmas*, costing £148, and that this sold out very quickly. Another popular item is the 3-D Christmas train, retailing at £125. Jonathan tells us all of this with a straight face.

If we *have* to have stuff from America, why can't we only have the good stuff? Can't we just take *Babylon 5*, Charlie Brown, JD Salinger, choc-chip ice cream and The Killers – and leave the rednecks to enjoy their burgers, their fries, their obesity, their charmlessness, their idiot president and their gung-ho, yee-hah, let's-save-the-goddam-world foreign policies without making them feel they have to share them with the rest of us? Do they also have to foist on us their idea of taste and restraint and their total lack of self-awareness and irony? After all, we'd only just started forgiving them for Garth Brooks.

The people that walked in darkness...

It's a way of life for some, which just makes it harder to understand for those of us who would see Satan skating past the front door before we would deck our houses in such tasteless gaudiness.

Let's have a closer look. It seems snobbish, but is unfortunately true, to observe that the abundance of external decoration is in inverse proportion to the social standing of the area. Thus:

- **Double-gated mansions:** sport a single wreath (probably handwoven from ethically sourced leaves) on the front door, just like the houses in the Victorian scenes on Christmas cards.

- **Neat suburban semi:** might stretch to a few hopeful-looking lights at the end of the garden, maybe a Santa or two. You get the sense that there's a bit of a domestic going on about whether to have them up at all, and that this is a compromise to placate the kids.

- **Row of council houses:** will be dripping with lights, stars and flashing animated objects, plus possibly a giant illuminated Virgin Mary. Gardens will be adorned with an army of eerily glowing snowmen, reindeer and hideous Santa Claus effigies, all illuminated with enough power to run the national grid of a small Third World country.

These monstrosities are presumably put up for the delight of a particular brand of children. They are the very same urchins who, two months earlier, adorn themselves with black plastic bin liners and glowing fangs and take a delight in knocking on all the doors in the neighbourhood in search of free confectionery.

Yes, for our ancestors, no terror was greater than the darkness of Hallowe'en night: the boundaries between this world and the next would grow thin and the restless and vengeful spirits would roam abroad seeking souls for the netherworld. In the twenty-first century, these have been supplanted by restless and vengeful pint-sized hooligans (whose idea of roaming abroad is Benidorm) demanding sweets with menaces. This is progress.

They then go on to be found sitting outside Oddbins, propping up an old pillow topped with a football (on which a mask of Wayne Rooney has been precariously fixed) and asking for money on the grounds that this Frankenstinian hybrid resembles the leader of the Gunpowder Plot. A few days later, you will hear them whooping with joy while letting off a small arsenal of Scud missiles in your back garden until three in the morning. You somehow doubt that they are celebrating a failed attempt to destroy the Houses of Parliament.

And the problem is (to return to the point) such decorations are not even pleasant to look at – you can imagine them scaring the wits out of small children at night. The glowing snowmen, in particular, look as if they are poised to become animated like the main baddies in a spectacular seasonal edition of *Doctor Who*, eyes glowing with extraterrestrial light and broomsticks levelled as they spit deadly fire into the heart of suburbia.

The backlash starts here

Be warned – not everyone will appreciate your seasonal illuminations. In 2004, one Cotswold couple, Carol and Roger Knapp of Gotherington, were even sent a poison-pen letter about their Christmas lights. The Knapps received the anonymous letter after living in the village for nine months. It read: 'Your dull, ugly front garden and tacky tawdry lights fail to reflect our village image. Please do what you can to improve matters. Thank you.' The seasonally named Carol spluttered: 'I think it's bullying and intimidating and cowardly. My husband and I moved into our bungalow in March and have worked endlessly on it ever since. We must have spent £4,000 doing up the front and back gardens, putting in a patio, plants and fencing. And as for the criticism of the lights – it's a single white string of lights, not anything tasteless. Believe it or not, it's the first time I've ever bought any.' (Well, maybe that'll teach you a lesson or nine, Carol.)

There has to be an element of neighbourly rivalry here, a bizarre kind of peacock display. 'Look at our house! We've got *lights*!' Having electricity is, in this day and age, not something which you really need to boast about (well, maybe it is if you live in some parts of rural Northumberland, but that's about it). In the summer, there are men who compete to see who can display the largest St George flag during the football competitions and who can rev the loudest lawnmower. In the winter, they transfer their rutting-stag tendencies to the application of festive electrical power. Sadly, as their good ladies will attest, an element of compensation is in play, and so the size of their glowing Santa is bound to be in inverse proportion to their manhood.

In Germany, meanwhile, everyone displays tasteful white light bulbs in straight lines on their garden conifers, with not a ghastly illuminated Rudolph in sight. It must be something to do with the trains running on time. (Then again, you'd expect no less from a people who actually have a single word for 'to commit the offence of placing one's rubbish in an incorrect bin'.)

If it all really becomes too much, make your neighbours think you have gone completely mad by getting your revenge. In spring, celebrate Beltane with a large, inflatable stone circle and a glowing image of the Horned God on your roof. You never know – it may make them think twice next year.

A final twist. From deep in the Arizona desert comes this website:

www.redtongue.com/badxmas.html

The astonishing pictures featured here are testament to a deranged kind of inventiveness. In the middle of the scorching desert, where snowmen and icicles would look somewhat incongruous, the local residents 'trim up' for Christmas by sticking painted plywood boards in their front gardens. Look and weep.

Spot the Unnecessary Decorations: a game to play in December

You may like to score the houses on your street or on your journey to work as follows:

String of lights across window:	1 pt
Lights across porch:	2 pts
Lights running along garden fence and/or wall:	3 pts
Illuminated Star of Bethlehem on porch and/or roof:	4 pts
Terrifying fibreglass snow-person:	6 pts
Horrifying illuminated Santa and/or reindeer:	6 pts
Entire outline of house picked out in lights:	8 pts
Reindeer and sleigh, lit and parked on front garden:	10 pts

6

The Great Christmas Myths

Jesus

Okay. So this is the big one. Might as well start here and then we can't possibly offend any more people than we do first off…right? On the other hand, even if it might be a made-up story, it's our made-up story, and the idea of playing it down because it might offend certain groups of people is frankly ludicrous. If you want to celebrate Eid, Hannukah, Diwali, the Coming of the Great Cloud Being or any other festival that might take your fancy, then feel free. I'm not going to stop you.

Jesus's mum and dad were forced by a silly quirk of bureaucracy to travel miles from home and had to put up with the only meagre accommodation they could find. (A bit like today's parents trying to find houses in their chosen school catchment areas, then.)

Peace on Earth

There's a slight problem here. The various splinter groups, regions and countries who are beating and bombing the hell out of each other across the world don't stop doing it just because some tacky lights have gone up.

You can't quite see today's squabbling factions getting down to a friendly game of footie in no-man's land like the English and the Germans did back in the First World War. For one thing, a normal football match is almost as violent, hate-fuelled and xenophobic as your average armed conflict these days anyway. And for another, one of them would probably load the ball with Semtex, offer to let the other team have a little kick-about to warm up and then retreat to their own goalmouth, sniggering.

And closer to home, the Burberry-hatted chavs in the street don't put their lagered-up fist fights on hold. Indeed, Christmas just seems to be an excuse for more of the same. The ready provision of extra alcohol doesn't exactly help, of course; some people just see Christmas as an excuse to pile into their local watering hole and down an extra six pints before closing time. Perhaps pubs could counter binge-drinking by offering seasonal 'Misery Hours', in which you pay double for a pint?

Goodwill to all men / A time for giving

Right, since when exactly? Christmas just seems to bring out the mean, grabbing streak in everyone. Restaurant menus have a 50 per cent premium added, while holiday booking prices go through the roof. And don't even get me started on the mindless hordes in every department store.

Santa Claus

A myth in which, if you have children, you are expected to be complicit. Sometimes this is more difficult than it might at first appear. Bright children will start posing difficult questions, such as exactly how a portly gentleman like Santa Claus hauls his lardy frame through the chimney pots, down such a tight space and out through the electric fire. You find yourself having to make up all kinds of stuff about expandable chimneys and flip-open compartments, and before you know it you've created a whole set of sub-myths which you then have to remember for next time. Lying becomes so much harder when you can't keep it simple.

The worst thing about Father Christmas is that he isn't even a proper myth. Not in the form he exists now, anyway.

Obviously he is based on the famous Saint Nicholas, who allegedly liked nothing better than delivering gifts to the world's children. You can't help thinking that Nick – while trotting out on a cold winter's evening to deliver two thousand PlayStations to the snotty-nosed brats on the council estates and shovelling up the reindeer dung – would have felt he'd got a bit of a raw deal over this. At his lowest ebb, he probably sat there on someone's roof, shivering, cursing the bloody kids, knocking back the brandy and wishing he'd been made the patron saint of something a bit easier, like Lost Causes or Putting Your Feet Up or Sorting Out the Middle East Peace Process.

But the 'Santa' people worship at Christmas is based on an image created to promote Coca-Cola in the 1930s. Yes, his uniform isn't red and white for nothing, you know. Now, that might sound pretty corporate and horrible, but just think about it for a minute. Things could be a lot worse. What about a 'Fanta Santa' dressed entirely in orange? Or how about the 'Pernod and Black' Santa in purple? And if it hadn't happened in the 1930s, it could have happened a few decades later. Imagine if Santa had been appropriated and branded in the 1980s. There is every chance that he'd have been transformed into Ronald McDonald, gleefully dispensing Big Macs with every child's stocking and poking his smackable, sinister clown's face into every card and gift tag. Or in the 1990s, he'd have been bought body and soul by Bill Gates and turned into an interactive, downloadable santa.com, complete with cyber-reindeer which, when you gave them a simple instruction, formed a little grey box above their heads asking: 'Are you sure you wish to giddy-up? Yes/No'. And Prancer would suddenly stall in mid-air for no apparent reason and flash above his antlers an information box reading: 'Application Error 232: This Process Terminated.'

And here's one for all of you who are wondering how on earth to break That News to your children before they are told it by someone else. In April 2005, a controversial art exhibition by Glasgow School of Art student Darren Cullen was scrapped. Darren's project was to have been a huge billboard proclaiming: 'Stop Lying to Your Children about Santa Claus' and 'Santa

Gives More to Rich Kids Than Poor Kids'. However, signboard company Maiden refused at the last minute to host the installation. Twenty-two-year-old Darren claimed he wanted to 'highlight the evils of consumerism', although one may suspect that Darren was motivated more by a desire for self-promotion than any sort of altruistic social conscience. He is probably planning his next installation right now – a 16-foot-high sculpture denouncing the Easter Bunny. Meanwhile, the Tooth Fairy was unavailable for comment.

7

The Father Christmas Letters

A is for... Angst

Joyous time of year? Do me a favour. December is the cruellest month – dark, miserable, full of fake snow, fake joy and tinsel. Guaranteed to send anybody's blood pressure soaring. Yes, the amount of stress you will experience at this time can be comparable with that of moving house. If you are planning to move house over the Christmas period at all, by the way, then you should perhaps seriously examine your sanity. And if you really are one of those people who's laid-back at Christmas, then I'd suggest you have residual traces of soft drugs in your bloodstream.

B is for... Batteries

The Plain English Campaign (PEC) has been claiming that people are finding the packaging on their Christmas gifts omits certain important details – including assembly time and whether or not the item needs batteries.

PEC spokesman John Lister said: 'At Christmas you can't buy something, open it up straight away, and get details of anything that's missing. If you give somebody a gift and you've already opened up the packaging they're not going to be very happy.' (Well, no – especially if it's a box of Thornton's chocolates and you've helped yourself to one or two of the best ones.)

So look out for those telltale little words: 'batteries not included'. If you don't, then you will face the wrath of a screaming child. Or, depending on what the item is, a very frustrated wife/girlfriend.

C is for... Church

Have you noticed how a lot of towns and villages sport these big, greyish stone buildings with imposing towers? All right, so many of them now house community centres and 'luxury accommodation portfolios' (or flats, as they used to be called). There was a time, of course, when they would ring to the angelic sound of children's voices and symbolised joy to the world, sanctuary and peace on earth.

Yes, one or two things happening at Christmas try to remind you that it's about a bloke who was born 2000 years ago, including the odd church service and a few bits of religious programming.

You may well be a committed Christian, one of the one million regular churchgoers in the UK. Or you may just have had a baby, in which case you're trying to get your face known before you dare to approach the vicar and ask about a christening. There's nothing worse than having a priest turn to you at the font and saying, 'Sorry, who are you again?' Or you may be a parent of a school-age child, and you've found that the local faith school is the only one in the district where the kids don't carry flick knives, deal drugs in the playground and leave at 15 to go on the dole – and so you desperately, meekly swallow your atheist pride, dress up in your Sunday best and troop along every week for a year in order to get that all-important letter from the vicar.

The odds are, though, that Christmas morning will be the one and only time a year when you actually dare to venture inside that big, scary building. Now, in any other week, going to church as a non-believer is an odd experience, especially if you choose a particularly lively one. It's akin to going to a football match when you don't like football and have no emotional involvement in either of the teams playing. It's also like going to an early-90s rave where everybody else is off their face on Ecstasy and having a great time, while all you can see is a cold, muddy field full of people dancing like lunatics to some tuneless, bleeping, ear-assaulting techno. You look around thinking: What the hell is going on? What on earth is everybody else *doing* here, and what is it they can see that I can't? Is there something fundamentally at odds with my view of the universe? *Am I a weirdo?* At Christmas, though, you can be reassured that a lot of you will be in the same boat. You'll spot the people who come every week – they'll be the ones sauntering through in their casuals, having a cheerful chat to the minister and generally looking totally at home there. Everyone else will be looking at their watches, hoping they get out before lunchtime and wondering if there will be any carols they know.

I'll go with my usual response, and maintain that the only church I fancy this Christmas is Charlotte. And leave it at that.

D is for… Decorations

If you really must have them, then put them up about 23rd December and take them down well before 6th January. They start to look a bit stupid after New Year anyway.

E is for… Escape

Longing to get away from it all? There are worse things you could do. If you have the kind of family that expects you to do the same thing every year, it's worth shaking them up a bit by announcing on 1st December that you intend to spend this year's festive season sunning yourself on a beach in Tenerife. And good luck to you.

Don't fall for that old trick of thinking it'll be a great idea to have a UK Break in one of our top hotels. You'll find yourself paying double the usual rates to eat processed turkey with coachloads of blue-rinsed bridge players.

F is for… Faff

Finding the end of the sellotape, and needing fingernails like Joan Collins to pick it off. Unravelling that crinkly stuff to go round the presents. Hoovering up the pine needles. Finding a way of sticking the cards up on the wall. Endless lists. And all that sort of thing.

G is for... Goodwill

Something of which you will need bucketloads. Alternatively, just don't bother and be a complete curmudgeon, which is easier.

H is for... Hallelujah

What you say when it's all over. Although if you think things get better, think again. Dr Cliff Arnalls of Cardiff University has produced a formula with which he has calculated that the most depressing day of the year is, in fact, exactly one month after Christmas Eve, on 24th January. Dr Arnalls cites the weather, debts and failed resolutions as people's main reasons for lapsing into despair at this time. Correspondents from Scotland have pointed out that it doesn't really apply to them, as they have the jollity of Burns' Night on 25th January to look forward to. Nothing like a bit of haggis to shake off the post-Christmas blues, apparently.

I is for... Invitation

You may be invited to socialise over the Christmas period, but it's as well to resist the temptation. It's bad enough that you will be accommodating your own extended family. The thought of having to nibble cheese straws and sip sherry with everybody else's will drive you over the edge. Manufacture some sort of excuse if you feel able – something contagious is always a good one, but try to make it believable (smallpox is perhaps overdoing it a little).

J is for... Jubilo

As in 'In Dulce'. Representing exactly the opposite of the way you will be feeling once you have staggered home laden down with electronic goods and wrapping paper and that Iceland advert is on for the fifteenth time, and you face the prospect of having to make small talk to Uncle Cyril about his operation.

K is for... Kids

Small terrorists. They want you to do what they want, or they will unleash chaos with their Weapons of Mess and Destruction. And *they* can do that in a lot less than 45 minutes, too. It is pointless trying to pretend they are reasonable human beings. Don't even think about trying to enter into negotiation with them – that way lies heartbreak, frustration and years of broken promises. Will make Christmas hell.

L is for... Liquid

As in refreshment. Much-needed if you are going to get through the whole thing. For some odd reason, people feel the need to break out the sherry at this time of year. Why you should want to inflict upon yourself a tipple that looks and tastes like alcoholic cough mixture is beyond me. Save up the decent wine, and crack it open when the first guests arrive. For yourself, that is.

M is for... Mistletoe

One of the most dangerous plants to have in your house – it has poisonous berries which can cause hallucinations. The ancient druids believed mistletoe to be an indicator of great sacredness. The winter solstice, called 'Alban Arthan' by the druids, was, according to bardic tradition, the time when the chief druid would cut the sacred mistletoe from the oak. The mistletoe was cut using a golden sickle on the sixth night of the new moon after the winter solstice. A cloth was held below the tree by other members of the order to catch the sprigs of mistletoe as they fell, as it was believed that it would have profaned the mistletoe to fall upon the ground. The chief druid would then divide the branches into many sprigs and distribute them to the people, who hung them over doorways as protection against thunder, lightning and other evils.

The druids believed that the berries represented the sperm of the gods, as they exude a white, semen-like substance. Mmm, tasteful. Because of this, my source informs me, the plant was thought to be 'a magickal aphrodisiac'. Quite why the extra k is required is a matter for conjecture. But it seems apparent that a girl carrying a sprig of mistletoe in her handbag is asking for a bit more than a snog.

As if that wasn't enough, the plant – also known as Allheal – was believed to cure everything from infertility to epilepsy, poisoning and the effects of witchcraft. It was also a plant of peace, and if enemies met beneath it in a forest, they would lay down arms and maintain a truce until the next day. (Presumably it was then in your interests to get up first in the morning.)

According to the Anglo-Saxons, kissing under the mistletoe was connected to Freya, the goddess of love, beauty and fertility. These days, if you are unfortunate enough to work in an office and doubly unfortunate enough to be forced to attend the Christmas party, you'll find sprigs of the stuff being brandished by balding, sweaty men called Keith and Alan, in the vain hope that they'll get a snog and a bit of a grope from Julie the secretary or Lesley in IT Support. Little do they know that both of these ladies would rather have their own toenails removed without anaesthetic than entertain the thought of physical contact with either of these gentlemen. Even when Lesley has had enough mulled wine to make amusing photocopies of her body parts, she still has some standards.

N is for... Nuts

Nobody buys nuts at any other time of year. And you can see why. They are one of the few foodstuffs for which the effort expended in preparing them to eat is completely out of proportion to the nutritional value gained. Your average hazelnut is bad enough – a carapace like hardwood floor-covering, concealing something small, chewy and nasty – but just wait until you get to the brazil nuts, which have been known to double as ammunition in several small South American armed conflicts.

O is for... Orange

Always ends up at the bottom of a child's Christmas stocking when parents run out of inspiration.

P is for... Pudding

A highly dangerous concoction dispensed to the family to round off the traditional Christmas meal. As if it's not enough trying to singe Granny's eyebrows by trying to set the thing on fire, you then have the fun of seeing who's going to be the first to choke on those little silver 'charms' hidden inside the mixture.

Q is for... Queen

Old woman who sits on her backside most of the year and delivers a patronising 10-minute homily to us Ordinary Folk on Christmas afternoon. Time for all republicans to switch off, or over to Channel 4. Alternatively: once-great rock band combining killer riffs with great melodies, fabulous pomposity and a healthy streak of self-mockery, and who now, despite having more money than Switzerland, insist on continuing – unable to see that they have become a pitiable parody of their former magnificent selves.

R is for... Reindeer

Rudolph is actually female. Seriously. In all the Christmas-card images, the best-known reindeer has antlers. But in real life, male reindeer don't sport antlers at this time of year. Allow me to explain. Antlers are weaponry – they are used for fighting with other males during the mating season earlier in the year. Afterwards, male reindeers' antlers fall off and don't grow again until the spring. Let's not even get into the theories about 'Rudolph the Eunuch', or half my readers will be crossing their legs.

S is for... Supermarkets

You're not seriously planning to make your own mince pies and Christmas pudding, are you? Get a life. Nobody will appreciate this, and unless you live in a strongly Republican, Bible-bashing, stay-at-home-soccer-mom suburb of America, it won't be expected. It's what Mr Sainsbury and the rest are for.

T is for... Turkeys

A turkey was spared when he was won by a vegetarian couple at a church Christmas raffle. Unfortunately, Ray and Maura Stroud from Somerton in Somerset, then found that there was nowhere in their small suburban semi-detached to keep their new resident, whom they had nicknamed Bert. The Bristol-based animal welfare group Viva! (exclamation mark compulsory, we think) came to the rescue; its director Juliet Gellatley agreed to adopt the bird. She probably ate a roast butternut squash for Christmas dinner, or something equally joyless. Meanwhile, all over the country, millions of other people tucked into their roast turkeys.

U is for... Underwear

Yes, it's the one time of year when a man will venture into the hallowed portals of Agent Provocateur and La Senza. Or rather, shuffle in.

V is for... Vaunting

A popular activity at this time of year, especially among those who send the obligatory Christmas circulars. This forces others either to ignore the self-congratulation, or to invent sufficiently impressive details about their own lives in order to compete. You'd think the whole country was full of 6-year-olds reading fluently in French, 13-year-old violin prodigies and students gaining A* grades in every exam they take while working in soup kitchens and spending their holidays learning to become scuba-diving instructors. Meanwhile, the grown-ups have nothing more important to communicate than the news of their latest tiling or carpeting venture. They must also always mention the purchase of a brand-new car, whose colour, model, engine capacity and accessories must be described in painstaking (and painful) detail.

W is for... Wenceslas

That daft Bohemian king who was into going out to help peasants gather winter fuuu-el.

X is for... Xmas

Well, what else? Don't you get annoyed when you hear the festive season referred to by a name that sounds like a skin complaint?

Y is for... Yule log

It's a chocolate sponge. Big deal.

Z is for... Zonked

So, as we established, Santa's traditional red-and-white costume is supposed to have been invented by Coca-Cola in the 1930s. However, a wacky alternative theory suggests that the outfit is meant to symbolise a variety of magic mushroom, identified by a distinctive red cap and white speckles. This idea – probably put about by dodgy hippy types trying to justify their permanent state of self-delusion – is based on the very dubious premise that villagers in Lapland used to indulge in funny fungi, in order to blot out the horror of the long dark months before they invented alcohol. Now, stop reading here if you are eating.

The story is almost credible, until it gets to the point where it suggests that the villagers would seek out places where the local shaman had relieved himself and eat the yellow snow in order to get traces of the proactive. Rrrrrright. I think somebody's been overdoing the sherry. We'd better get back to that story of the Star in the East and the little bloke in the stable, which is slightly more believable…

8

Needles and Pins

A couple of weeks before Christmas, you go for a drive around the supermarkets, looking for blokes with trailers sporting clusters of uprooted fir trees. You then pore over the collection of sorry pines, looking for the one which looks the least misshapen and droopy, before handing over an exorbitant amount of money to the bloke with the trailer.

There then follows a scene likely to be in the comic style of Laurel and Hardy or Mr Bean, in which you attempt to cram a 6-foot-tall piece of foliage into a small car patently not designed for the purpose. This will usually involve folding down the top bit, and/or squashing the entire thing out of shape as you attempt to cram it in between the front seats and the kids. Ignore screams of protest from the back as small loved ones are scratched and lacerated by vicious needles.

At the other end, the item is hauled out of the car and into the house – still trailing needles – by which time you are already swearing blind that you'll buy an artificial one next year.

And then you find it's too big.

This can't be true. You were assured by the bloke on the trailer that it was a 6-foot tree, and your living-room ceiling can't be any lower than 7 feet or there are at least two of your friends who would be braining themselves on the lampshade every time they came round to visit. But no. The door is there, and the tree is here, and one refuses to admit the latter. It just isn't going to happen. Not unless you mutilate it.

You need to snip it with the secateurs, only you can't find them so you end up attacking it with the kitchen scissors instead, which produces an effect rather less like topiary and more like some kind of expressive sculpture. After the thing has been levered into position, blocking out all available light in the room, it wobbles there, leering at you like some demented spiky version of a triffid.

And then you have to decorate it.

The Christmas lights, assuming you can even find them, will obey the same laws of physics as a garden hosepipe – i.e. no matter how carefully you rolled them up when you put them away the previous year, they will have mutated over the course of the year into a tangled mess. Once you have got them straight and draped tastefully over the tree, you'll switch them on and find that they're not working, and so then you have to test each and every bulb in turn to find out which one is the offender.

After you have got the lights sorted out, there is the small matter of the other decorations. First of all, if you take a step back from them, you realise what an odd concept they are. At no other time of the year would you consider draping your living room with huge, reflective baubles which look like the bastard child of Puff Daddy and Bet Lynch. Then there are the chocolate things: how paltry are they? The foil comes off if you so much as look at them, the chocolate itself is wafer-thin and tastes only slightly nicer than old cardboard, and the only way to get them on the tree is to tie the threads together into a loop, a job so fiddly that it makes your hands feels if they are twice their usual size and encased in boxing gloves.

Once the thing is up, decorated and lit, there's nothing to do but sit and look at it. And, as if in acknowledgement of its derisively inert state, the tree invents something to do so as to keep you occupied. It moults. Pine needles drop in their thousands from its branches, forming a crunchy circle of green on your carpet. They skulk in the skirting and you are still picking them out of the upholstery at Easter.

You have to ask yourself – what on earth would a man from

Mars (or, indeed, Chris de Burgh's Spaceman who Came Travelling) make of this very odd custom? The humans buy a giant piece of foliage, they haul it into an unsuitable space, prop it up in a container, cover it with plastic-and-metal adornments, drape it in small illumination and watch the needles drop from it. Then, a couple of weeks later, they strip the foliage bare again, haul it back outside and leave it on a compost heap somewhere to go brown. All across the country, trees which were at the epicentre of the house now lie in ditches, forgotten and abandoned like the seasonal revelry.

Is it really worth the trouble? You can't help thinking you'd be better off with one of those giant plasma screens that show a restful image.

9

The White Stuff

When snow first starts, it always turns people into gibbering idiots as if they have never seen any before in their lives. They gravitate to their office windows and stand there gawping, watching it cover the roofs and cars as if it's the most exciting phenomenon on Earth. Then again, in this country, it is pretty unusual, and therein lies the crux of the problem – we just don't know what to do about it. People start to panic, leaving work early; schools and offices have to close because of frozen pipes; traffic banks up on the M1 and cars are abandoned. It's as if Britain turns into some grim scene from a Jerry Bruckheimer post-Holocaust film, and all because of a bit of weather.

Our European cousins accept that the weather is part of the daily routine, and are prepared for it. In the Black Forest in Germany, heavy snow can be a fact of life from November through to March – people dress sensibly, their cars have snow-tyres and snow-chains and their gritters are out and about early. Here, it's a wonder if you ever see a gritter at all, and even then you're lucky if they do any more than the main bus routes. And if you open one of those yellow bins marked GRIT on your street corner, which the local oiks have helpfully relabelled with another four-letter word, you'll find it either empty, or full of festering dog turds.

Then there's the fact that people, even those who have garages, like to leave their cars on their drives, or even the road (probably because their garages are full of the accumulated clutter of their lives and the paraphernalia of their hobbies). So you get up, bleary-eyed, and as you're making yourself that first cup of coffee of the day you happen to glance out of the window and see everything covered with a thick layer of white. You allow a choice profanity to escape your lips and get dressed hurriedly, mentally adding half an hour on to your morning journey. Out you go, swaddled in coat, scarf, hat and boots and armed to the teeth with brush, de-icer, scraper and (should everything else fail) a bucket of hot water. You trudge to the road, where the car is parked. You set to work. You brush the snow from the roof, bonnet and windscreen so as to expose the crisp layer of ice below. You get going with the de-icer and the scraper, trying to ignore the slow numbing of your hands. After about ten minutes, you may have cleared a gap on the windscreen just about big enough to see out of if you were to crick your neck into an awkward position. You scrape some more, making a token effort to clear some space from the side and rear windows. Then you step back from your handiwork, checking your watch, reassuring yourself that you haven't lost too much time after all. Your breath mists in the air and you feel an oddly warm glow, a sense of satisfaction. And then you realise you have been scraping the ice off next door's car.

They don't always get it right on the Continent, though. In Germany, the local residents of suburbia are almost fetishistically attentive to shovelling the snow out of the way, sweeping their paths clear and removing the snow from the area of pavement in front of their doors. This, conveniently, gives the surfaces the texture of polished glass. Really clever. What's doubly ironic is that, if you don't ascribe to this convention of making everybody's pavement a skating rink, you get the usual round of hard stares and tutting.

So please don't tell me you're dreaming of a white Christmas, just like the ones you used to know. There are very few people left alive who will remember a proper white Christmas anyway. Christmas Day is always neither one thing nor the other in weather terms – it usually manages to be steel-grey outside, with perhaps a bit of wind and rain, as if Nature is grudgingly accepting that nobody's going to be venturing outside as they will all be slumped in front of *Only Fools And Horses*.

The USA didn't exactly have a great time of it at Christmas 1998. Driving snow across the north-east, freezing rain throughout the south and north-west, airports becoming emergency shelters, power lines freezing and snapping... Roads became impassable. In Nashville, 500 people spent a night on the bus station floor or in parked coaches. 'If you prayed for a white Christmas,' said Kurt Pickering of the emergency management agency in Tennessee, 'you should have been more specific.' Well, quite.

10

Who the Hell Are Jeff and Sandra?

n these days of email, texting, wi-fi and goodness knows what else, does anyone actually use the postal service for communicating with friends at all? Well, of course, they do at Christmas. An email card just doesn't cut the mustard.

You'll probably have seen that there are cards available for all sorts of occasions. You can mark everything from 'Sorry to hear your auntie's goldfish died' to 'Congratulations on your decree absolute'. But Christmas is still the biggest time of year for the vendors of small folded pieces of card in envelopes, and so this is why you'll start to see the racks being cleared for them around August.

First-class greetings

The best kind of cards are those from people you see maybe three or four times a year, such as friends or relatives in other parts of the country, because there actually seems some point to them. A brisk message of goodwill followed by a couple of informative sentences is really all you need: 'Hope you all have a good one! We'll be doing the usual turn at the soup kitchen, followed by an afternoon at Grandma Maud's. Not even started the shopping yet! Looking forward to seeing you in Feb. Love, Jonty & Jess.'

But some make you wonder why they bothered.

The third most pointless sort of Christmas cards are from people you see every day, such as your work colleagues – why not have a charity collection instead?

The second most pointless are those from that couple you met ten years ago on holiday in Majorca who you only made friends with because they had children of about the same age, and who you realised once you got home that you couldn't stand, but who have kept in touch with you ever since and keep threatening to turn up on your doorstep with a boxful of slides.

The most pointless are those from people you don't even know. Once, long ago, you may have bought some paper from PaperWorld. Every Christmas since then, you have received a faceless, corporate card with a fake signature in that horrible 'handwriting' script which makes you think it's been produced on a computer last updated in about 1994, saying, 'A Merry Christmas from PaperWorld to all our valued customers!' I have no idea why on earth I should want this, or be heartened or inspired by it, or why it will make me more likely to buy stuff from PaperWorld again in the future.

Then there are the cutesy cards with the family posing on the front beside the Christmas tree, all in matching jumpers, with the father behind in the role of Victorian paterfamilias, his hand proprietorially on his good lady's shoulder. The Blairs send this kind of card. It's up to you whether you want to be like them.

Technology has brought the wonder of the email card, the preferred seasonal method of communication for people who don't even want to bother writing your name on a piece of card and putting a stamp on the envelope. If you're on dial-up, you'll spend twenty minutes fuming as you sit there waiting for the thing to come in, only to find it's a two-dimensional dancing robin on some pixellated snow, sent by somebody you barely remember who you were at school with twenty years ago.

Within all these categories, there are those which send you either too much or too little information. Later on, we deal with the joys of the 'Christmas circular'. Here, we shall pause to mention those inexplicable cards which are simply signed with the names of the senders and reveal no further clues as to their identity. 'Happy Christmas. Jeff and Sandra.' Or: 'Season's

Greetings. Mike and Helen.'

Your other half comes down the stairs as you are opening the post.

'I see we've got a card from Mike and Helen,' you say quickly, hoping not to let on that you don't know who the hell they are.

'Oh,' says other half, then: 'Who?'

You affect irritability. '*Mike and Helen*. That's Mike who you work with, isn't it?'

Moment of arm-folding. 'No. Mike's gay, remember? It's Mike and *Ralph*.'

You frown. 'Oh. Well, maybe it's Helen from Basingstoke and her new boyfriend.'

Pause. 'If it's Helen from Basingstoke, why would she sign it "Mike and Helen" and not "Helen and Mike"?' demands your other half, not unreasonably.

You shrug. 'I don't know, do I? Perhaps he wrote them all.'

'Well, anyway, it's not her. Her boyfriend's called Justin, and they sent a card last week.'

You have a think. 'I know. That woman you used to work with years ago, at what's-it-called. She was a Helen.'

'She was an *Ellen*. And she was a Jehovah's Witness. She didn't celebrate Christmas.'

You have another think. 'Your mum's Great-Uncle Michael?' you hazard.

'Er, no. He never called himself Mike in his life. And he's been dead for six years.'

'Really?'

'Yes. Really.'

'I wondered why he hadn't sent us a card for a while.'

You continue like this for a while, and eventually have to admit that neither of you knows anybody called Mike and Helen. You can only conclude that you have been the recipient of a random act of Christmas-card sending, perpetrated by someone who gets a bizarre kick out of picking total strangers out of the telephone book and sending them cards in order to flummox them.

Here's a final nugget for you: the World's Worst Christmas Card. *Private Eye* came up with this, the card signed by the East Midlands Conservative EuroTeam – including Tory MEPs Chris Heaton-Harris and Roger Helmer. It featured a beaming Santa astride a reindeer singing: 'Ho Ho Ho, not Euro-Ho!'

11

All Present and Correct

Consumer society is not shy at the best of times, but at Christmas it rubs its hands with glee and begins opening the vaults. People start getting a strange glint in their eyes. There's no logical reason why this should be the case. The idea that this orgy of purchasing has its roots in the Christian story is patently absurd. It may have been a while since I read anything biblical, but I'm pretty sure there's no bit in the Gospels where Melchior, Balthazar and Caspar frantically pile on to the camels to get down to Al-Hadji's Emporium in order to grab the last decent gifts on the shelf, and are foiled by some determined fat woman who elbows them out of the way with a screech of, 'Move, sunshine! Our Joshua's been on at me all year to get him a pot of frankincense, and I ain't gonna let you stop me now!'

Neither do we see them facing a sneering bazaar-owner who, in between counting his shekels, laughs sarcastically at the thought that they might get what they are looking for at this time of the month. '*Myrrh?* You gotta be jokin', ain'tcher? Sold outta myrrh two weeks ago. Ain't gettin' no more in till after the New Year, mate. You shoulda got it on order back in November.'

And you can't really imagine the Three Wise Men sheepishly turning up with some socks, a couple of joss sticks and a tub of bath salts. 'Look, I'm sure he'll like them when he's tried them out. I know it's not what he wanted, but have you *seen* the crowds in Jerusalem? We're going to do all our shopping by carrier-vulture next year.' Meanwhile the shepherds offer their lamb, risking sarcastic comments about how far they must have had to go to get that.

And it isn't really documented what Jesus did with all his, er, wonderful gifts. I mean, I suppose Mary put on her best smile and said, 'Ooh, frankincense, lovely; that'll be good for getting rid of the smell of cowshit in the manger.' And I imagine that, by the time the toddler JC was up and walking, he had the gold strewn all over the living room and was painting the walls with the myrrh. And Mary was there going, 'I don't care if you are the Son of God. If you do that once more, you'll be spanked and sent to your room.' Then she'd lose it and call in first-century Palestine's equivalent of Dr Tanya Byron from *House of Tiny Tearaways*: 'I don't understand it. *He's* controlling *me*. I mean, don't get me wrong, I love him and I know he is the Messiah sent to bring Light to the World and all that, but some days I could just clout the little bugger round the earhole.'

It's the thought that counts

So here we are, two thousand years later, supposedly replicating the gifts given to the Christ-child by finding some horrible socks for Uncle Bert which are just like every other pair of horrible socks he owns.

Or: by agonising for ages in the underwear department of M&S, wondering how to find the wife something which looks like neither an insulated tarpaulin made for pulling in excessive amounts of blubber, nor a cheesewire-tight thong designed to be displayed by a pair of baggy jeans hanging halfway off a pair of tattooed hips and whose purpose is to draw attention to the wearer's impressive collection of abdominal piercings. The time you can spend doing this without the security men deciding you are actually a pervert and throwing you out is approximately twenty-two minutes and thirty seconds.

Or: by desperately browsing all the identical scarves in H&M and wondering if there is one which is neither too patterned nor too plain for Aunt Minnie, and wracking your brains to remember whether you actually bought her an H&M scarf last year.

Or: by taking your courage in both hands and entering the Early Learning Centre or the toy section of John Lewis, picking your way through all the Tarquins and Jemimas who are choosing their own rocking horses and interactive train-set complexes and wondering if you can find some way of guessing what a 9-year-old niece or nephew would like. This is complicated by the fact that they will probably laugh scornfully at the sort of thing you and your contemporaries would have happily enjoyed playing with yourselves as 9-year-olds, like Swingball sets and skipping-ropes and Action Men and Hula-Hoops. They are meant to be more sophisticated now. By the age of seven, they've started experimenting with make-up and lipstick and earrings – and the girls are just as bad. (Sorry, I did try to resist that, but I just couldn't.) On the other hand, these days they tell us forty is the new thirty (you're desperately clinging on to that thought as you look in the mirror each day), which means that thirty is the new twenty and twenty is the new ten (a view borne out by observing the behaviour and general intelligence levels of 20-year-olds with whom you are familiar), which means that… It makes your head spin.

Or: by venturing sheepishly for the one and only time in your life into the hip-hop section of HMV. You do this in order to buy your 14-year-old cousin an apparently essential double album which you have to find on the shelves and take to the till, even though it features an arrogant-looking, excessively bejewelled young black man in a vest, reclining on the white leather seats of a Cadillac and swigging cognac with a bevy of busty beauties – and which you dare not ask for by name, because it happens to be called something like *Da Posse An' Da Pussy* and has song titles along the lines of 'Gonna Fill Ma Bitch Wi' Da Lead From Ma Shotgun Dick, Suckaz'.

If you are a man, you may decide after about an hour that you have spent a pretty long time on this shopping lark – more than enough for one year – and that what you have got will probably do. If you are a woman, you will have spent three hours darting in and out of shops, being distracted from your mission by several new items of clothing which you wish to try on and emerging at the end with precisely nothing bought for anybody else.

Catalogue gifts

The cop-out option. Whatever would possess you, at any normal time of year, to browse through a selection of ornamental bottle-stops, decorative tea cosies, fake stone birdbaths and hand-held games involving ball bearings? Do your family really want these things or are you so devoid of imagination that you simply can't think what else to buy them? The thing about catalogues is that they exhibit a kind of cosy vulgarity – they legitimise naff. In no other circumstances would you think it acceptable to buy a relative an oven glove embroidered with their initials, or a set of pencils embossed with their name. Then there are the small 'executive' playthings which, if they were made of plastic, would be on sale in Poundland, and yet which are given a veneer of middle-class respectability simply by being made of polished wood. It's odd the way the British psyche works at times.

Um, thanks, Dad...

Every year there is a concerted joint effort by the media and a toy manufacturer which would shame the publicity departments of most political parties with its dedication to 'spin'. It's an attempt to get each and every parent in the land to believe that there is such a thing as this year's 'must have' toy. Whether it's a Buzz Lightyear, a Star Wars light-sabre or an Android My Little Pony, the race is on from early November and the shelves are clear by mid-December. Yes, one thing that the dreadful Arnie Schwarzenegger film *Jingle All The Way* gets right is the shop-owner's derision at the idea that the parent might just pop in on

Christmas Eve to pick up one of these desirable items.

There are shortcuts, but you use them at your peril. One year, not long ago when we had the first *Thunderbirds* revival (back when Busted were still in nappies), the toy which all children had to have for Christmas or else risk being the laughing stock of the class was a Tracy Island. The ever-enterprising *Blue Peter* showed its viewers how to make one for a tenth of the price, assuring mums and dads that the kiddies would not be able to tell the difference. Up and down the land, kids opened their presents and looked in despair upon an Anthea Turner construction of foil, washing-up-liquid bottles and sticky-back plastic.

Bring it all back

Yes, there is always the inevitable gulf between what children want on Christmas Day and what they actually get. Those of us old enough to remember *Multi-Coloured Swap Shop* will recall that it used to thrive on children's attempts to undo the misguided generosity of relatives: 'Gary from Walsall has a set of Superman socks and an Action Man with one arm, and he'd like to swap them for a full-size *Star Wars* Imperial Stormtrooper and a ZX-81.' Noel Edmonds would then chuckle beatifically and invite people to call on 01-811-8055 (it's seared into the memory of most thirtysomethings, that number) if they could help. They usually couldn't.

There used to be, for the sake of decency, a lull between Christmas and the January sales, a cooling-off period in which people could reflect on their seasonal stupidity and queue up to return those unopened socks, duplicate copies of books, handwoven tea cosies and Chris de Burgh albums. But no. These days, there is no let-up. The January sales, in what might be perceived as a mild infringement of the spirit of the Trades Descriptions Act, now kick in on Boxing Day. That's right – December the twenty-sixth. That traditional day of recuperation and respite – which used to be a time for taking long walks, eating cold turkey sandwiches, watching *The Empire Strikes Back* and hiding the batteries for the more annoying of the children's toys – is now the first day back at the shops, a day on which the feeding frenzy begins again.

Families descend on furniture warehouses, spurred on by those ever-so-agreeable adverts featuring the lovely and not-at-all-smackable Linda Barker (whose voice is not at all like the sound of fingernails being scraped down a blackboard, oh no). Some of them obviously think it's been named Boxing Day for pugilistic reasons. You'll find yourself battling with old women whose elbows have been honed to a fine stabbing point over years of practice doing this kind of thing, and who will show no mercy as they viciously force you out of the way in that stampede to the reduced bath salts and the bargain-price kitchenware. As you queue for hours, sweating under the striplights and sandwiched in between a boisterous family of six and two nattering pensioners, you do start to wonder if there are better ways of spending one of your precious bank holidays.

Sometimes, you may even find yourself going out for a bargain and unexpectedly getting a riot thrown in for good measure (witness the scenes in January 2005 at the opening of the Edmonton IKEA). Good news for those who thought they'd have to go and see some New Year football to get their fix of violent action.

12

Logs on the Fire and Gifts on the Tree...

Or maybe it should be the other way round?

It's incredible how such a time of supposed goodwill can engender feelings of antipathy and resentment not found at any other time of the year. There will come a Christmas – if it hasn't come already – where you will ponder your pitiful pile of presents and wonder how on earth it came to this. Three shirts, a paperback and a mug? Is that it?

If you have children, this realisation will probably coincide with their first or second Christmas – their haul of loot will increase exponentially as yours decreases. Some people think children make Christmas a joyous occasion, but they are obviously living in a fantasy land where all children are a cross between those on Victorian Christmas cards, those in *It's a Wonderful Life* and the little darlings in St Winifred's School Choir. If you have ever physically witnessed a demented 4-year-old let loose on a pile of presents on Christmas morning, you soon learn to shake off any such illusions.

The worst presents anyone can give, according to a recent survey, are:

Cheap perfume: Obviously, this one is a non-starter. It's no good buying your good lady a bottle of something which could easily double up as paint-stripper. It's saying to her, 'Look, I think you ought to smell a bit nicer, but I'm not prepared to get you any decent Yves Saint Laurent or anything, because, basically, it's a bit overpriced. And anyway, you're not as fit as the French birds.' Yes, telling her you don't like her bodily scent is bad enough, but asking her to cover it up with something from the bargain basement of TJ Hughes is even worse. Be prepared for it to be poured down the loo, and for you to be sleeping in the spare room.

Handkerchiefs: Since when did these become things which it was acceptable to give as presents? When you consider what they are actually used for, it rather brings you down to earth. Presumably you wouldn't give someone tissues as a present? Or toilet paper? Even when embroidered with amusing motifs, handkerchiefs are still predominantly an item for hygiene. Don't be fooled by the attractive box.

Socks: More often, 'wacky' socks – often featuring cartoon images designed to subvert the sobriety of the work-suit. Again, the choice of item seems somewhat…utilitarian.

Novelty jumpers: A jumper is a useful item at Christmas. Simple equation: British weather is brass-monkeys and jumpers are warm. However, if you get one decorated with stars, kangaroos, rainbows, teddies or goodness knows what else, the purchaser is under the impression that you are either a) someone with a highly developed sense of irony, b) so boring that you need something like this to replace your personality, or c) Gyles Brandreth. To be avoided at all costs.

Trampolines: Excuse me, what? Yes, trampolines. Because they are extremely dangerous, apparently. People put them in gardens that are too small for them (that would mean pretty much everyone's garden, then) and the number of under-15-year-olds with fractured bones, cracked heads and dislocated limbs caused by trampolines has apparently increased fourfold over the last five years. 'The most common injuries are caused by collisions and bouncing off the equipment', apparently, which if you like can be translated as 'the most common injuries are caused by stupidity'. Apparently the craze was started by the Inuits, who liked to toss each other around on walrus skins. The six-month-long winter nights must just have flown by.

However, these only orbit the outer circle of the truly cringe-inducing. Digging deeper, we find a list which suggests potential 'worst' gifts along gender lines, as follows:

MEN

Books and videos on the subject of erectile dysfunction: Look, he won't want to be reminded of this little problem, especially at this time of year. It's bad enough that he has to endure the jokes about Father Christmas only coming once a year.

The 'Razorba' back shaver: Apparently it's the only way to remove your back hair without enlisting the help of another person. Such a thoughtful gift.

Anti-flatulence pills: Again, a probably pragmatic but rather less than romantic gift.

Nose-hair clippers: You're really telling him you love him, aren't you?

Penile 'enhancement' products: Not the best way to put him in a manly mood for carving the turkey. It also appears to have been inspired by the items in his email spam-trap. Next you'll be suggesting you buy him a direct debit to a West African bank account, some online Viagra or a book of 'XXX Big Busty Bulgarian Lesbians'. (Actually, he probably wouldn't mind the last one.)

WOMEN

Diet products: All right, so she will probably be moaning all through the Christmas period about how much weight she is putting on. You, on the other hand, are not allowed to mention it at all, on pain of death.

Jenna Jameson's Pubic Hair Trimmer: Not, you will understand, an item for trimming the lady-garden of Jenna herself, but one 'endorsed' by her. Yes, in the spirit of Paul Newman's sauces, the George Foreman Grill, Carol Vorderman's Detox Diet and fitness videos from soap stars galore, here's the tie-in from 'adult' film star Jenna Jameson. How to tell your girlfriend 'you need to pay more attention to keeping it tidy down there'. I don't think so.

Breast firming cream: And let's face it, you're not really on to a winner with this either, are you?

Anti-cellulite products: Same with these, really. The thing with men and cellulite is that you have to pretend *you don't even know what it looks like* – in fact, that you are unaware of its existence. Because, of course, you've never seen any – right?

Vaginal moisturisers: And this just goes beyond the personal and into the downright insulting.

Shop-brand menopause pills: Tell your beloved that she's over the hill and having all kinds of odd things happening to her. It's about as subtle as saying to people that you no longer need the radiator on as you feel quite toasty sitting next to her hot flushes. And look at you – getting the shop's own brand! You really know how to push the boat out.

Gimme Gimme Gimme

Extensive research has been done in the Worst Gift area, and a national survey was undertaken in 2003 to see just how horrifically out of control the whole business had become. Nominations included the following. All are absolutely true, but names have been changed to protect the guilty. The reason all of these things are so wrong is that we, as British people, should want to do anything other than commit the ultimate, cardinal sin – *causing embarrassment.*

- **Best Use of Dramatic Irony:** A tobacco tin engraved with the initials of the recipient, 43-year-old Mike – who had given up smoking some months earlier.

- **Most Unreliable Memory:** A bumper colouring book – given to 31-year-old Jim, whose elderly aunt now had difficulty remembering how old he was.

- **The Argos Award for Being Pragmatic, But Not Terribly Exciting:** Sylvia received ten thermostatic valves for all the radiators in her house.

- **The Poundland Award for Being Pragmatic, Not Terribly Exciting and Useless:** A less than delighted Marcus got a multipack of drill-bits. He is a confirmed DIY-hater and has never possessed a drill.

- **The Heartbreaker Prize:** Twenty-six-year-old Rhiannon received a framed wedding photo from a couple who were friends of hers; unfortunately, she is still in love with the man in the photo and, to this day, cannot bear to look at the picture.

◉ **Special Prize for Mistaken Identity:** Sarah, 29, who often expressed her liking for singer Robbie Williams, was a little flummoxed when she opened her gift from her grandmother – and found DVDs of the films *Mrs Doubtfire*, *Flubber* and *Dead Poets' Society*.

◉ **The 'Caught Out' Award:** Jennifer, a 40-year-old Hertfordshire housewife, received a hairdryer from her mother-in-law – not a bad gift, but unfortunately identical to one she already had. On taking it back to the shop, she was told it would be no problem to exchange it; all they had to do was get the product information from the barcode and Jennifer would be given the equivalent value in vouchers. The staff duly scanned the barcode, revealing that the hairdryer was one which had been given away in a free-gift promotion earlier that year. Oops.

13

Jesus Loves Your Money

Even those of a pious bent are not, apparently, exempt from this orgy of giving – in fact, they have been some of the worst offenders when it comes to tacky presents.

Yes, it should come as no great surprise to find that, at this materialistic time of year, the godly community is into profits as much as prophets. So here's our top-ten rundown of the best consumer items which Christian entrepreneurs – presumably in a spirit of 'if you can't beat 'em, join 'em' – have produced for the festive season. Each and every one of these is true. Believe me, I wouldn't have made them up.

For Dad & Mum

Bobbing Jesus: Not a profanity, but the worshipper's answer to the nodding dog; it sits there in the back of the car with its arms out, ready to embrace any driver who shunts you up the rear. (And you thought 'God is my Co-Driver' bumper stickers were bad enough.) I wonder if it casts its beatific spell over you as you stand there berating the other driver for their ineptitude and casting aspersions on their parentage? You could always get a cross-shaped 'Jesus On Board' thing to hang on the back as well. I just made that up, and I now have a horrible, sneaking feeling that it may well exist in reality.

For Kids

The 'God Thinks You Are Special' Plate: A piece of pottery in lurid red, inscribed with this comforting thought. This is the kind of thing which only brain-dead, Bible-thumping, right-wing

America could have come up with. Why the hell does God think you are 'special'? What's he going to do, invite you to come up and be his apprentice? Oh, apparently, 'Your kids will love the attention and you'll love the way their face lights up!' No, your kids will think you are a cheapskate and will say, 'A *plate*? Where's my bloody Xbox?'

For a Happy Couple

The Bouncy Church: Bookings have not exactly been buoyant for this ecclesiastical answer to the 'fun castle', available to put up anywhere in the country for impromptu weddings, funerals and christenings. You've got to admire the idea – people weren't coming to church, so church would come to the people. I'd imagine you've got to be careful hammering up those parish notices, though. All flaws aside, I'm surprised it's not caught on. You'd think it would have inspired such imitators as the Bouncy House (put up in a matter of seconds in the desirable street of your choice) and the Bouncy School (now you can be sure of being in the catchment area).

For Grandma

The Crying Santa: In homage, perhaps, to lachrymose statues of the Virgin Mary across the world, your porcelain Father Christmas is an original addition to any bathroom or guest bedroom. Not only sheds tears, but does so to the strains of 'O Come All Ye Faithful'. Accompanying 'Weeing Rudolph' surely only a matter of time.

For Little Brother

The 14-inch 'Jesus Loves You' Beach Ball: Stand and sob as it floats out to sea and you wonder whether Jesus Doesn't Love You Any More.

For the In-Laws

Adam & Eve Cruet Set: Those naughty misbehavers from the Book of Genesis are lovingly recreated as salt and pepper. A short step from Commandments to condiments, and only £19.95. This seems like just the start of something bigger. Maybe we will next get the Cain & Abel Matching Fruitbowls, the Lot's Wife Salt Pillar and Abraham's Sacrificial Carving Knife (Ideal for Firstborn Sons).

For Teenager

'Smile, Jesus Loves You!' Magnetic Dartboard: I hope someone is thinking what I'm thinking here. Sadly, it just features a smiling sun and a rainbow.

For Toddler

The Genesis Teether: Sadly, not a chewable item adorned with the faces of Phil Collins, Mike Rutherford and Tony Banks, which plays 'Invisible Touch' when salivated upon. This is for the young churchgoer in your family – a teething ring inscribed with 'Jesus'. But why stop there? Surely super-absorbent nappies featuring the face of Judas Iscariot are a must (and just 30 pieces of silver to you, my son)? Or face flannels on which the face of the Virgin Mary only appears when immersed in water? And how about a high chair inscribed with the Ten Commandments, with a few more added for good measure (e.g. 'Thou shalt not throw thy Food at Mum and Dad, thou little Bugger', and 'Thou shalt not wake up at some ungodly Hour of the Morning')?

For Executive Uncle

The Evangecube: 'Looking for an evangelism tool that's fast, fun and focused? Check out Evangecube! Reminiscent of the Rubik's Cube, the Evangecube will help you walk friends through the Gospel presentation using pictures. Flip one way, and show man's separation from God. Flip again, and you'll see Jesus stepping from the tomb.' Like Rubik's Cube, only adapted to convey some illustrations of biblical teachings. (Bizarrely named as 'Best New Resource for Children's Outreach' by readers of *Outreach* Marketing Magazine.) There is an Evangecube Keychain and Dangler too. Woo-hoo! Coming soon, no doubt, the Twelve Apostles version of 'Connect Four' and the 'Man's First Disobedience' edition of 'Downfall'.

For the Couple Living in Sin
Ten Commandments Blanket: A touch of morning piety. Presumably giving them bedclothes with 'Thou shalt not commit adultery' emblazoned on them will make them mend their wicked ways.

For the Young Man About Town
Floating Cross Boxers: Manly undergarments featuring crosses on a background of heavenly blue, perhaps intended to send out the message that you may be a Bible-basher but you are still virile.

For Little Sister
The 'My Best Friend, Jesus' Plush Doll: About as far into 'you couldn't make it up' territory as we are prepared to venture. Looks worryingly like Demis Roussos. Oh, and he's got blue eyes. Which really tells you everything you need to know about American right-wing fundamentalism. On similar lines is the camp-looking 'My Sweet Jesus' doll: 'not only soft and comforting, he's also a wonderful reminder that Jesus is with us always. Even if we just need a hug!' You can also get 'Jesus Action Figures', which just sound so…*wrong*.

14

Thank God It Isn't Christmas
Every Day

Delighting in all manifestations of the Terpsichorean Muse

Last Christmas, I gave you my heart, and this year, to save me from agonising pain, I'm just going to forget the whole thing and have beans on toast – OK?

Every year, the pop charts seem to lose control of what few senses they have remaining and to throw all vestiges of credibility to the icy northern winds.

There is nothing worse than a party with no booze, where you are wedged in between two ugly people and forced to listen to someone else's rubbish music compilation while being enticed to dance by a crap DJ in horrid comedy spectacles. For some reason, this nightmare scenario was taken as the template for *Top of the Pops* in the mid-1980s.

Furthermore, the audience were forced to throw streamers, wear 'Santa' hats and cavort among industrial quantities of dry ice and Jabolite. One could have forgiven them all for turning on Mike Smith and Simon Bates in a horrific Christmas Day Massacre. Of course, it never happened, not even when the Pogues and Kirsty MacColl, after making officially The Best Christmas Song Ever, failed to reach the top slot in December 1987.

And if you think it all starts horribly early – well, you're not the only one. Even the perpetrators sometimes have second thoughts. In November 2003, Jimmy Lea from Slade had a few words to say about 'Merry Christmas Everybody' being on the radio for weeks, even months before the festive season. Jimmy observed: 'You don't start singing "Happy Birthday" to somebody two months before the day. Please don't start playing it again yet. I don't want to hear it for at least another month.' Jimmy then actually went even further in his denouncing of the Christmas market, saying that he was withdrawing from it all. 'I'm no Scrooge,' he said, 'it's just that I'm sick and tired of the Christmas hysteria. I think it's ridiculous.' Well, Jimmy, you'll find no argument here.

Because of that remarkable piece of self-awareness, I'm going to be kind to Slade and leave them off the list which follows. Presented below, however, is the ultimate Christmas compilation – the one which will make the December suicide rate rocket and find travel agents doing a roaring trade as music fans seek to escape the nightmare Britain has become. We proudly present:

The Worst Christmas Album In the World... Ever

Track 1   Spice Girls 'Christmas Wrapping'

What's sadder? A good band dumbing down for the festive market (hello, Queen) or a bunch of Wannabes™ pillaging Christmas Past to create their own horrible spectral images? The most ugly cover you'll see this side of Auntie Mabel's sofa, this is more scary than Geri Halliwell coming over all macrobiotic and vegan and doing the splits, and not realising she was far sexier when she had a bit of meat on her. Get out the Waitresses' original, for goodness' sake.

The only redeeming feature about this recording, meanwhile, is that it *isn't* the very worst Spice Girls song: that plaudit must surely go to their final chart-topper, 'Holler', a crashingly tuneless piece of R'n'B wailing and thumping which was really just a single too far.

These days, Scally, Tubby, Common, Bimby and Pointless are safely scattered to the four winds and pursuing their own separate interests in footballers, exercise and tuneless rock. However, you can confidently expect them to be squeezing back into the spangly catsuits and little black dresses for the inevitable 90s revival – which will be happening any time soon. Stay tuned.

Track 2   Cliff Richard 'The Millennium Prayer'

Ah, Sir Cliff. Saviour of middle-aged women everywhere, the Peter Pan of pop (although I don't believe he has ever actually been known to fly). As much a part of Christmas as the cheap sherry and the depressing *EastEnders* special. Here, he loses the plot, jumps the shark and goes down the plughole with the home-made plonk. If you thought David Bowie doing the Lord's Prayer at the Freddie Mercury tribute concert was a low, you hadn't seen anything. Putting this prayer to this song must count as the most embarrassing thing you can do on your knees (short of being Monica Lewinsky). Congratulations (and celebrations) to Cliff for doing the unthinkable – making Auld Lang Syne even more cringeworthy and unbearable. And to think we were going to let him off for doing 'Saviour's Day'.

Track 3   Mr Blobby 'Mr Blobby'

There is a rumour that well-known disc jockey Noel Edmonds does not own a record collection. Listening to this, it's not hard to believe. Yes, the children of 1993 were happy to be serenaded by a large pink phallus with yellow blobs on. Just because he was invented by an obscenely cheerful man with a big beard – who happens to have been born on Christmas Day – that doesn't make him festive.

Track 4   Whigfield 'Last Christmas'

Here's your career. Here's its natural lifespan. Funny how some people can't take the hint, isn't it? Whigfield – alias PVC-clad bimbo Sannia Carlson from Denmark – offered this diluted take on an already quite insipid Wham! song before fleeing these shores for good, with no sign of her ever returning. Boing, boing, boing. Di-di-na-na-na to you too.

⊞ Track 5   Wizzard 'I Wish It Could Be Christmas Every Day'

Anyone who wishes it could be Christmas every day clearly has psychological problems of a kind which cannot be addressed by dressing up in big boots and declaiming as much on television and radio. This clearly deranged desire for a kind of festive *Groundhog Day* is obviously the result of overcompensation for some kind of childhood trauma. I can only suggest a short course of aversion therapy, beginning with a frantic trip round the Lakeside Centre at Thurrock to buy presents for all the family at 4 p.m. on Christmas Eve.

⊞ Track 6   Shakin' Stevens 'Merry Christmas Everyone'

Shaky forgoes his usual retro denim gear to put on an avuncular jumper and sit by the fireside, dispensing wisdom over a glass of mulled wine. The song chugs along with all the dynamism of your gin-soaked gran staggering to the Roses box. It rather makes you long for Mr Stevens' bequiffed cut-price Elvis days, when he only used to sing about old houses, green doors and ladies called Julie.

⊞ Track 7   Queen 'Thank God It's Christmas'

A lesser crime compared to many, but it's not exactly 'Bohemian Rhapsody' or 'A Kind Of Magic', is it? Sadly, in these days of post-Freddie exploitation of the good Queen name, Brian May and Roger Taylor have a shedload of further musical travesties to be ashamed of, including collaborations with Wyclef Jean and Five. (Just what are they *doing*? They can't need the money.)

⊞ Track 8   St Winifred's School Choir 'There's No One Quite Like Grandma'

A patently fatuous assertion, boys and girls. In later life, as they queued at the post office on a Monday morning behind a dozen

OAPs claiming their pension, or attempted to go shopping at 4 p.m. on a Friday, they will have realised that, in fact, the world is full of people like Grandma. Still, at least they knocked John Lennon off the top spot, for which their place in history is assured.

▓ Track 9   Craig 'At This Time of Year'

Remember the dawn of 'reality' TV? For about five weeks back in 2000, chirpy Scouser Craig Phillips was taken to the bosom of the country for exposing 'Nasty' Nick Bateman and eventually triumphed over lesbian skateboarding nun Anna and dull Darren to become the first-ever UK winner of *Big Brother*. Of course, it's entirely possible that you don't give a toss about *Big Brother*, which is commendable. It also means that you have probably never heard Mr Phillips' bid for the Christmas 2000 Number One slot, for which I envy you. Someone, somewhere clearly went mad as a result of too much sun and, excited by the burgeoning phenomenon, signed builder Craig up for a five-album deal.

Why, we may ask in passing, do entertainment bods assume that someone who is famous in one arena (although, I'd admit, winning *Big Brother* is stretching the definition of 'famous' just about as far as we can) will automatically demonstrate transferable skills, such as they are, and flourish in a totally different area of showbiz? The evidence for the prosecution: the acting career of Jennifer Lopez, the pop career of Minnie Driver, the literary efforts of Naomi Campbell… It's funny how nobody signs up writers for this kind of vanity project. Just imagine – we could have had Nick Hornby's blues covers album, Martin Amis's stint presenting *Have I Got News For You* and Jeanette Winterson on *Non-Entity Shagging Island*. Hmm, perhaps not.

Just finally on Craig – it's worth noting that, had he fulfilled the five-album promise, he would just about now be gearing up to release his answer to *The Joshua Tree*. Thankfully, the record company execs finally saw sense when this seasonal single stiffed at no.14, and Craig slipped into rent-a-builder daytime TV mode.

🎁 Track 10   Boyzone 'Father and Son'

Not released specifically as a Christmas single (it came out in November 1995) but hung around for sixteen weeks like a particularly strong cheese. The Irish quintet give this rather sensitive song enough of a mauling to make Cat Stevens/Yusuf Islam reconsider his commitment to love and pacifism.

And it's from the time when Ronan Keating, presumably under the impression that he was the reincarnation of Johnny Rotten, sported enough gelled-up spikes to put someone's eye out. We are also treated to his trademark vocal acrobatics, pitched somewhere between a growl and a squeal and unfortunately making it sound as if he is singing without his teeth in.

🎁 Track 11 Cliff Richard 'Mistletoe and Wine'

Sir Cliff, of course, is always associated with festive records, despite the fact that he only had a couple in the Sixties before this one. 'Mistletoe And Wine' is from back in the days when he still sported a kind of mullet, and could quite happily walk around in big Mike Read glasses and a shiny blouson jacket of the sort usually favoured by ostentatious racing drivers.

Mistletoe, Sir Cliff might like to know, was traditionally collected on the ninth day of a new moon by a druid dressed in white, who would cut it with a golden sickle and catch it on a white sheet held by maidens. Traditionally, one's chances of conception are meant to increase if mistletoe is tied to your good lady's ankles and wrists while making love. You can just see this forming the basis of a dance routine at Cliff's latest Wembley concert.

Yes, this is the song where the world's most famous Christian pop star sings a perplexing homily to the joys of an alcoholic beverage and the seasonal fertility plant, not to mention the logs on the fire and the gifts on the tree. Not a patch on 'Saviour's Day', though – but somewhat better than the ghastly version of 'Somewhere Over the Rainbow' which he inflicted on us later in his career. That's so bad it makes the Eva Cassidy version sound good. For some inexplicable reason it turns into 'Wonderful World' halfway through, as if Cliff couldn't quite make up his mind which song he most wanted to cover and decided to hedge his bets. So look out for this year's Cliff offering, in which he returns to his rock'n'roll roots and performs a medley of 'Anarchy in the UK', 'Frosty the Snowman' and 'Smack My Bitch Up'. It's predicted to be kept off the top slot only by a ringtone of the *EastEnders* theme performed by a bunch of dancing monkeys.

Track 12 Whitney Houston 'I Will Always Love You'
Houston, we have a problem. You have just shown the world how to make a dreary song even drearier. The fact that it was at Number One for ten weeks in the UK, stretching across Christmas and New Year, made it seem all the more tedious at the time. The last note goes on for *ever* and will have all the cats in the neighbourhood scrabbling at your door.

Track 13 The Smurfs 'Your Christmas Wish'
Where are you all coming from? And can you please go back there, as soon as possible?

Track 14   Mariah Carey 'All I Want for Christmas is You'
Let's face it, if you could choose to be uniquely desired by a queen of pop at the festive season, who might you choose? Kate Bush? Debbie Harry? Perhaps even the lovely Andrea from The Corrs? Anybody, one might suggest, but the conspicuously under-talented Ms Carey, a warbler who is never content to use

one note where an entire arpeggio will do. Her video features a festively hatted Mariah snogging a reindeer. She's then seen descending a snowy hill in a toboggan at what looks to be a promisingly alarming rate, followed by an impact with a snowdrift. However, to the chagrin of music lovers everywhere, she recovers and goes on to record hideous duets with tone-deaf leprechauns Westlife.

Even more terrifyingly, there is a 2002 album, *Merry Christmas*, on which Mariah openly slays various unfortunate carols, bumping them off in more imaginative ways than were ever dreamed of by the writers of a *Midsomer Murders* Christmas Special. And you don't even get the pleasure of slamming the door in her face.

⁂ Track 15   Chris de Burgh 'A Spaceman Came Travelling'

'On his ship from afar', no less. Listen in growing horror from somewhere behind a cushion as the Eyebrowed One sings of the joys of Christmas reinterpreted as a low-budget sci-fi movie. For some reason, either Chris or the spaceman is under the impression that a 'light year' is a measurement of time. The worst bit of all is where *it-builds-up-to-a-big-chorus-and*: 'it goes, Na, Na-na, na, na-na, na, na-na, naaaaa…' Incessantly.

Don't forget, this is the man who brought us 'Lady In Red' in 1986, possibly the worst number one ballad of all time. He's now a sort of cross between Neil Diamond and Daniel O'Donnell, with a worse haircut than either. But on the other hand, this is also the man who wrote the sublime 'Spanish Train' and 'Waiting For The Hurricane'. It saddens me to see how far he has fallen.

⁂ Track 16   Madonna 'Santa Baby'

A misguided Christmas song from the Queen of Pop, and as such it ranks even lower in her canon than 'Hanky Panky'. Surely she could have done an iconoclastically offensive version of 'Mary's Boy Child' instead? Or maybe it was meant to be 'Satan Baby' and she chickened out on the eve of a Bible Belt tour? Whatever the truth, this is just an awful song. 'Come and trim my Christmas tree', anybody? Er, no thanks. And the henna tattoos and Kabbalah bracelets just don't do it for me, Madge.

⚏ Track 17   East 17 'Stay Another Day'

So relieved were the compilers of the charts to have a half-decent song at the top of the seasonal Top 40 in 1994 – let's not forget this was just a year after 'Mr Blobby' – that pop historians have seized upon this averagely good ballad by the London quartet and reinvented it as a classic. It's overplayed and overwrought, and given a festive flavour only by the gratuitous addition of bells in the closing bars. The baseball-hatted boys, normally happier to be bouncing around and flashing their bling on upbeat anthems like 'It's Alright' and 'House of Love', looked distinctly uncomfortable when performing this, their first and only number one, on *Top Of The Pops* amid the obligatory flurries of dandruff-like plastic snow.

⚏ Track 18   John Lennon 'Merry Christmas (War Is Over)'

Ready to slaughter a sacred turkey this Christmas? Let's go.

It's a toss-up between this and 'Wonderful Christmas Time' by his old mate Macca, alias Lord Beatle of Bootle, but this is marginally worse. 'Merry Christmas (War is Over)' – alternatively, 'Happy New Year (No It Sodding Isn't)' – tops a dismal solo career. It's a jolly little singalong number, in which John, Yoko (what exactly is the *point* of Yoko Ono?) and a bunch of smackable children warble a mawkish hymn to peace. Perhaps John had his head so far up his own backside by this time that he was oblivious to the range of international conflicts still raging while his song zoomed up the charts. (Contrast with 'I Believe in Father Christmas' in which Greg Lake cynically observes 'the Christmas we get, we deserve'.)

Yes, it is quite difficult to keep an eye on world events when you are closeted in your plush country pad being a tortured genius, proclaiming yourself bigger than Jesus and counting your royalties. Don't forget this is the same man who had the brazen cheek to invite us all to imagine having no possessions, while sitting at a white grand piano in the lounge of his enormous mansion. Rrrrrright. Then there's all the effort of growing a ridiculous hippy barnet while taking to your bed for six years, surrounded by all the security money can buy to make sure no nutter runs up and shoots you.

Oops. Spot the problem there.

⚏ Track 19   Michael Ball 'When a Child is Born'

Ah, the singular Mr Ball. Following the peak of his chart promise with 'Love Changes Everything' in 1989, he backtracked somewhat and became a bouffanted balladeer and singer of show tunes for ladies of a certain age. Mr B lends the power of his unique tonsils to this rendition of the 'classic' made famous by Johnny Mathis. This is what today's manufactured popstars could become. Look upon him and tremble, Will Young.

⚏ Track 20   Jive Bunny & The Mastermixers 'Let's Party'

No. Please. Let's not.

The saddest thing is, I know some evil person out there will be downloading each and every one of these and burning them to a CD as they read this. Please, don't send it to me. (If you do, perhaps I can put them into that inexplicable section on the Windows Media Player called 'Music Tracks I Dislike'.)

As a side note, here's a preview of the track which might outdo them all to become the worst Christmas number one of all time:

'Walkin' In Da Air (DJ Urban Snowman Mix)'
Performed by Aled Jonez Featuring MC MuthaF**kin Bastard

[Backing: Ba-booma-boom DOSH,
ba-booma-boom DOSH throughout.]

MCMFB:
Yo, goin' out to da Snowman masseeev,
Keepin' it real ONE time
Check DIS out!

Aled:
We're waaaaa-lking in the air!
We're floooo-ating in the moooon-lit skyyyy,
The peee-ople far bel-ooooow are sleeeee-ping as we fly.

MCMFB:
Yo, yo, wad I say? Christmas Day, here we go, man,
Walkin' in da air like da muthaf**kin' Snowman,
Walkin' in da air like da man of snow,
Flyin' in da sky wid ma bitch an ma ho!
Me heart iz pumpin' an I feel it in ma bonez,
Sing it for me one more time, ma homeboy, Aled JONEZ!

Aled:
We're waaaaa-lking in the aaaaaa-ir!

(MCMFB:
Uh-huh. Ah yeah.)

Aled:
We're fl-ooo-ating in the moooooooon-lit skyyyy!

(MCMFB:
One time! Two time!)

Aled:

The peee-ople far bel-oooow are sleeee-ping as we fly.

(MCMFB:

People dey a sleepin', nobody a peepin'.)

Aled:

I'm hooool-ding very tiiiiiii-ght,
I'm riiiiiii-ding in the miiiiiiid-night bluuuue,
I'm finding I can fly, so high above with yooooooou.

MCMFB:

Walkin' in da air, lookin' down on da town-uh,
Got so high, never gonna come down-uh,
Christmas in da hood, sing about baby Jee-zus,
Peace on da Earth, man, dat gotta pleez us.
One time, two time, wid ma homey call Aled,
Sing da Snowman song, it's a funky li'l ballid!

Aled:

We're waaaaa-lking in the aaaaaa-ir!
We're fl-oo-ating in the mooooooon-lit skyyyy!
The peee-ople far bel-oooow are sleeee-ping as we fly.

MCMFB:

Yo, yo, yo, keepin' it real at Christmas, man.
Peace an' love goin' out to all ma bruthaz.
Give it up for ma homey, Aled!

Aled:

Safe, man. There's lovely.

15

Figgy Puddin' an' All That: a true account (part 1)

KNOCK KNOCK KNOCK.

Wife: Door.
Me: Leave it.

KNOCK KNOCK KNOCK!

Wife: Aren't you going to answer it?
Me: It'll be bloody carol-singers. If I want to hear ugly, talentless kids dementedly caterwauling for the sole purpose of parting us with our hard-earned cash, I can watch *Pop Idol*.

KNOCK!... KNOCK!... KNOCK!

Me: Oh, for God's sake.

Stomp-stomp-stomp. *Creeeeeeeeeeak.*

Me: Yes?

[At the door, four sullen, spotty youths in Sheffield's traditional festive garb: i.e. hooded tops, baggy trousers, trainers and baseball caps.]

Youth: Carol-singers, innit.
Me: I beg your pardon?
Youth: Carol-singers, innit. [Urchin holds out grubby hand.]
Me: Have you actually grasped the point of this exercise?
Youth: Yer waat?

Me: I mean, you know you actually have to *sing*, right? This isn't like Penny for the Guy or Trick or Treat. You do actually have to *do* something.

> [Urchins glance nervously at one another and grin.
> Collective body language says 'we got a rait one 'ere, ain't we?']

Me: So go on, then. Entertain me. *Sing*.

> [Nervous shuffling of feet. Nudging and laughing,
> a bit of shoving in the ranks. After a few seconds, two of the youths
> break into uncertain, almost-in-tune, *a cappella* version of 'Stay
> Another Day' by East 17.]

Me: That's not a Christmas carol.
Youth: It fookin' is. It's on me mam's fookin' Christmas CD, innit?
Me: Get lost.

SLAM!

16

Figgy Puddin' an' All That:
a true account (part 2)

KNOCK! KNOCK! KNOCK!

Me: Yes?

[Bunch of reasonably well-scrubbed children on doorstep.
Immediately break into fractured version of 'We Wish You a Merry
Christmas'; predictably, they sing 'to you and your *king*'. During
chorus, one of them answers his mobile phone. When they finish,
there is an expectant silence.]

Me: Yes, yes. Almost in tune, as well… So, do you know what that
carol is about?

[Worriedly look at one another. One of them shakes head.]

Me: What – nobody? Didn't they teach you in school?… Do you know
what the bit about 'Glad tidings we bring' is actually referring to?
Child: [nervously] Is it…like…all them people what you want to say
Happy Christmas to and that?
Me: Nope. Try again.
Another child: It's, like, all that stuff about people what you was rude
to during the year, like yer nan. And you gotta be nice to them and
have them round for Christmas even though you can't stand 'em.
Me: No. Come back when you've found out the answer.

SLAM!

[Two days later.]

KNOCK! KNOCK!

[Small girl on own, from previous group, is standing at front door.]

Me: Yes?
Small girl: Summat to do wi' Jesus.

[She gets fifty pence.]

Me: Now go and buy some sweets. And don't come back.

SLAM!

17

The Best Ways to Deal with Carol-Singers

(In ascending order of probable effectiveness.)

- Have a sign on your door saying 'No Carol-Singers'.
- Have a sign on your door saying 'Carol-Singers Must Die'.
- Have the television on very loudly.
- Draw the curtains, turn off the lights and pretend to be out.
- Stand at the window wearing dark glasses and a hearing aid.
- Tell them you are a Jehovah's Witness and therefore don't celebrate Christmas.
- Pretend to be a foreigner who has never heard of Christmas.
- Ask *them* for money.
- Say 'Little boys, little girls, I can smell you! Come on in!' in your best Child Catcher voice.
- Say you don't have any money, but you can pay them in last year's brazil nuts.
- Come to the front door naked.
- Come to the front door wiping a kitchen knife on a bloodstained apron, and then invite them in.
- Set up water-cannon turrets linked to a tap inside the house, with which you can spray them with icy jets as soon as they start to sing.

✥ Come to the door looking wildly up and down the street, tearing at your hair and rolling your eyes, and saying, 'The voices! The voices! They're back again!'

✥ Set up a tape playing some evil-sounding backwards Latin and stentorian laughter, which goes off at the same time as an array of green lights and swirling dry ice. Then answer the door dressed as Death, complete with scythe.

Of course, you will do none of these. For you know one thing to be true. You know that if you do not embrace the money-grabbing spirit of the occasion and give the snotty little urchins something – even if it's only a couple of euros and some spare drachmas from 1993 in a sealed brown envelope – then you'll have the seasonal joy of finding slugs (or worse) being put through your letterbox. Or waking up to find that your car is adorned with the carefully scratched accolade of WANKER (how is it that normally illiterate youths have no trouble spelling anything vaguely profane?). Or that its wheels have been expertly removed and replaced by bricks. The only option is to continue lobbying your MP for compulsory, nationwide curfews on everyone below the age of 16, and be done with it.

18

Shoot the Sodding Partridge

The very worst Christmas carols and 'traditional' songs

Carol-singing is an old tradition dating back to ancient Greece. The name originates from the word *choraulien*, meaning 'to dance to a flute'. By the Middle Ages, 'carol' meant 'to sing and dance together', and by 1987 it had come to mean 'that frizzy-haired tart in Accounts who always wears Boots No.17 and white high heels'.

Over the centuries, the carol has become inextricably associated with Christmas. Even the fact that an encouraging number of them were banned by Oliver Cromwell hasn't been able to keep them down. More recently, other songs of dubious provenance have become known as 'traditional', which is really no guarantee of quality at all.

And then there are those creepy, insidious 'modern' carols, usually written sometime in the 1980s by happy-clappy Christians with jeans and earrings called Graham and Phil – all of which sound like the very worst, soulless MOR rock and are about as enjoyable as eating your own sick.

But let's have a closer look at the fifteen most tiresome examples of the genre – those which make you swear you will never again switch on the seasonal *Songs Of Praise* with Diane-Louise Jordan. As if you were going to in the first place.

15. 'Away in a Manger'
The carol which is designed to bring together two things which should be kept apart, like sprouts and marmalade, or roast beef

and rum sauce – namely, toddlers and singing.

Adults sit with rictus grins on faces while pre-schoolers burble their way through half-remembered words. You are then expected to clap as if you have just heard Lesley Garrett duetting with Placido Domingo. Each year, you remind yourself that this is why you are not coming to the crib service again. Each year, you go back.

14. 'Silent Night'
OK, so this is not too bad. You may know how it starts:

> Silent night! Holy night!
> All is calm, all is bright
> Round yon virgin mother and child,
> Holy infant so tender and mild,
> Sleep in heavenly peace,
> Sleep in heavenly peace!

But then you may not be so familiar with the version that carries on:

> Silent night! Holy night!
> Shepherds quake at the sight.
> Glories stream from Heaven afar,
> Heavenly hosts sing Alleluia,
> Christ, the Saviour, is born!
> Christ, the Saviour, is born!

Sorry, but the thought of all those quaking shepherds is stopping me taking this entirely seriously. Are they cold from being out in the fields in the middle of December, perhaps? Then, this odd alternative-universe take goes on:

> Silent night! Holy night!
> Son of God, Love's pure light
> Radiant beams from Thy Holy face,

With the dawn of redeeming grace,
Jesus, Lord at Thy birth,
Jesus, Lord at Thy birth.

Is it just me or is there no verb in that bit?

13. 'We Three Kings'

Endless verses, plus a chorus which you see coming each time with all the terrible inevitability of a Morecambe & Wise punchline. It doesn't help that, for three of the verses, the congregation has nothing to do but stand and listen. The verse with the myrrh is usually sung by a fearsome baritone in a minor key and must be designed to scare the pants off children.

This carol also takes the liberty of sharing the rather dubious information that the Journey of the Magi has included 'field and fountain' – for no better purpose than to find something to rhyme with 'moor and mountain'.

12. 'Silver Bells'

Oh, God, this is where it starts to get really awful.

Strings of street lights,
Even stop lights,
Blink a bright red and green
As the shoppers rush
Home with their treasures.

Excuse me, *treasures*? Since when? I suppose 'the chavs rush home with their Elizabeth Duke at Argos jewellery and their PlayStations' doesn't quite have the same ring to it.

11. 'Good King Wenceslas'

Look at it from the point of view of the page. He's just got his master's supper done and finished the washing up, and he's about to settle down in front of the fire for a good kip. Then in comes the mad King of Bohemia, burbling about some peasant who's stuck outside in the snow, gathering firewood. His Majesty, in an inexplicable burst of magnanimity, wants to go out there in the deep and crisp and even and help the poor bugger. Oh, great. Just what you want to do on a bollock-freezing December evening. Why didn't the page say, 'Look, sire, I appreciate your sudden need to come over all approachable and that, but it's brass-monkeys out there. And he's a *peasant*. Gathering winter fuel is what they *do*. And anyway, far be it from me to give advice, but if Your Majesty really cared so much about the subjects, Your Majesty could always consider abolishing the repressive feudal laws altogether and instigating a fairer system of democratically elected people's representatives?' Well, all right, maybe he'd have got his head chopped off.

Oh, and once again we get that mountain/fountain juxtaposition, for, one suspects, purely aesthetic reasons rather than those of historical accuracy.

But the very worst thing about this carol is that *it doesn't finish properly*. One minute the hapless page is following in his master's footsteps as he trudges through the very sod, and you think you're about to find out what happens when they get to the peasant who's caused them all this trouble – and then it ends. What? I at least want some pay-off here! Was the peasant grateful? Were their attempts to gather fuel in the rude wind's wild lament successful, or did they all freeze to death because of the mad monarch's sudden crazy impulse to help the poor of the parish? We should be told. It's as if the writer suddenly thought, 'Oh, bugger it, this is a stupid story, I can't be arsed any more.'

10. 'The Holly and the Ivy'
Yes, it's a song about plants – and not even edible ones. Medieval people used holly to protect against dog bites and measles, while

in the Dark Ages it was thought to be a talisman against witches. Ivy, meanwhile, is associated with melancholy because it is often found in cemeteries. Trust me, all of that is a lot more interesting than the carol.

9. 'Deck the Halls'

> Deck the halls with boughs of holly,
> Fa la la la la, la la la la.
> Tis the season to be jolly,
> Fa la la la la, la la la la.

Why, exactly? Who are you to advise me not only on matters of interior decoration but also on the correct State-imposed mood for Christmas? There is a distinct Stalinist agenda emerging here. And those bloody *fa la la la la, la la la la*s go on for ever.

8. 'The Wassail Song'

Now here's one which actually celebrates the New Year rather than Christmas. That may sound like quite a good idea until you actually hear it. Anybody who tries to come a-wassailing round here is going to get short shrift, I can tell you. Especially when you see this bit:

> We are not daily beggars
> That beg from door to door,
> But we are neighbours' children
> Whom you have seen before.

To which you'll reply, 'Yes, too bloody right I've seen you before, and yes, you are daily beggars, especially when you throw stones at my garage and play football in my front garden. Piss off!'

7. 'O Tannenbaum'

An ode to the Christmas tree, to the tune of 'The Red Flag'. What's this all about, then? Do you really feel the need to come over all worshipful at the sight of a conifer bedecked with metal baubles? Is your life really so hollow that you need to sing the praises of a gaudily decorated Scandinavian fir? And the amazing message of this tedious carol is – the tree stays green all year long. Big wow.

6. 'Ding Dong Merrily on High'

As if it didn't start horribly enough, there is that interminable chorus of 'Glo-o-o-o-o-o-o-o-ria…', not to mention bells being 'swungen' and lots of people singing 'i-o, i-o, i-o'. What the hell is this, a Dutch Eurovision entry?

5. 'Rudolph the Red-Nosed Reindeer'

You are supposed to embrace the concept of 'jolly' with this upbeat pre-New Labour paean to the joys of social inclusion. For those of us who don't really do 'jolly', it's not much fun. Basically, the plot is that the other reindeer are a miserable bunch of bastards who you would probably cross the tundra to avoid, and they won't let Rudolph join in any of their 'reindeer games'. It's never actually explained what might pass for entertainment in the reindeer world, but Rudolph is obviously suffering from self-esteem issues and has a burning desire to be accepted by the in-crowd. All it takes, it becomes clear, is for him to be suddenly elevated to the position of Santa's favourite and – bingo! – everybody wants to be Rudolph's best mate. It's about as plausible as the kid who's picked on in class suddenly becoming cool because he is made Register Monitor for a day.

4. 'Jingle Bells'

Taking inanity to new depths, here's yet another piece of God-awful singalong rubbish about Santa and his jolly four-footed helpers. It's a horrible piece of propaganda, too – 'oh what fun' it is to be pulled through the freezing countryside in a rickety wooden sledge by a crazed beast? Not if you've just had your Christmas pudding and a few glasses of mulled wine, it isn't. And have you *heard* the Destiny's Child version? Shudder.

3. 'The Little Drummer Boy'

The only song which actively entices adults to sing the words 'parum-pa-pum-pum' (and which is only saved from being the nadir of David Bowie's recording career by the existence of 'The Laughing Gnome'). And a little boy coming along and whacking a drum just as Mary has got the baby off to sleep – hmmm, will he really be all that popular?

This was voted the worst carol of all time by readers of the *Chicago Tribune*. 'With a musical range of exactly seven notes,' said one reader, 'and a scale-like melody that only a first-year piano student could love…this song is the musical equivalent of watching paint dry.' Other comments included: 'embarrassingly mawkish', 'lugubrious and schmaltzy' and 'repetitive and mind-numbing'. (Harsh words indeed, from a country that was quite happy to give us Billy Ray Cyrus.) Another agonised correspondent noted: 'Even when sung by children accompanied by an actual little boy playing drums, it's interminable.' Surely that 'even' should read 'especially'?

2. 'We Wish You a Merry Christmas'

If you really wanted me to have a Merry Christmas, you wouldn't inflict this tedious piece of musical criminality on me year after year. And no, I'm not going to give you any bloody Figgy Pudding. Go away. On the other hand, it's a positive work of genius when compared to:

1. 'The Twelve Days of Christmas'

The most tedious, brain-mulching piece of rubbish ever to find its way into a festive songbook, and enough to make you want to become a pagan. OK, so you know exactly what you're going to get – it doesn't take a genius to work out how many verses there are – and yet it just seems to go on and on and on for ever.

Each round adds a fresh layer of inanity into the mix. It's the aural equivalent of Chinese water torture. You start to go into a kind of trance singing it, bobbing your head from side to side and mouthing any old words, a bit like John Redwood on that embarrassing clip where he attempts the Welsh National Anthem.

At the four calling-birds stage, you're nervously glancing at your watch and hoping that you didn't leave the turkey on too high. By the time you get to those sodding pipers piping, you're gnawing your fingernails down to the quick and begging to be let out so that you can go home and watch *The Snowman* for the fifteenth time. Even the *French & Saunders Christmas Special* is going to seem fresh and original after this. People in the congregation have fallen asleep and died while singing this song. People have got engaged, married and divorced again between verses one and twelve.

Quite apart from anything else, it's completely stupid: what the hell is the recipient expected to do with this abundance of wildlife (some of which are, let us note, a-laying), not to mention the milkmaids and the hyperactive peers of the realm? Are you supposed to put all these uninvited guests in the spare room with Auntie Mavis? And does your true love seriously think that the five gold rings (the only decent present in among this lot) are going to make up for the turtle-dove guano all over your soft furnishings and the twelve drummers whacking the hell out of your hung-over head at 7 a.m.?

Let's be honest, though, even if someone rewrote the whole

thing for the twenty-first century to make the booty on offer more palatable – say two remote-controlled cars, five Terry's Chocolate Oranges and eleven DVDs – it would still be an utterly crap carol.

19

Supermarket Sweep

Just what is it with supermarkets and their obsession with piped music? It's bad enough at any time of year, but at Christmas you can double the agony. Do they think we are incapable of trudging the aisles without the accompaniment of a beat-box-and-flugelhorn version of 'Hark the Herald Angels Sing'? If deprived of the delights of a Hi-NRG version of 'I Believe in Father Christmas' ringing in our ears, would we be unable to make the right decision when it comes to choosing the best-value brand of Christmas pudding? Perhaps the theory is that, on hearing 'Jingle Bells' for the fifteenth time since Bonfire Night, our hearts will be so swelled with seasonal pride and delight that we will start to stack our trolleys even higher with festive provender.

It's doubly ironic if you happen to find yourself in Kwik-Save, Lidl or Netto, of course, or any of the other shabby pile-'em-high emporia of one-brand goods in which this country specialises – yes, the places that make you sure that the British food retail industry takes its inspiration from pre-*perestroika* Eastern Europe.

Once, stranded in one of these sad places and desperately looking for fruit juice, I forced myself to ask assistance from the uniformed 19-year-old girl with the Croydon facelift, trowelled-on make-up and oversized ear-bling. After staring at me for about five seconds, she took me to the next aisle and pointed to the shelf piled high with bottles of a popular orange substance.

'That's not fruit juice,' I said.

'Iss wot we got,' she countered.

'Yes, but it's not fruit juice. It's a small amount of orange flavouring mixed with water, sugar and tartrazine. It's almost entirely unlike fruit juice. You don't seriously think I'm going to give that to my children?'

She shrugged. 'Iss wot we got.'

Yes – goodwill to all men is the last thing you feel when you're shopping in a brightly lit bargain-bucket supermarket with sad-faced zombies whose idea of healthy produce is low-tar cigarettes. Looking around at the armies of the dispossessed grimly loading up their trolleys with blue pop, Mother's Shame bread and Special Brew, you do wonder how appropriate it is for the tannoy system to be belting out its proclamations of joy to the world, peace on Earth and kindness to little donkeys. One does start to feel that the events in Bethlehem over two thousand years ago are supremely unimportant to a populace whose priority in life is choosing the right shade of Burberry cap, voting in *The X-Factor* and getting to the Lottery till before it closes.

Or is it me?

Danger money

That's just the effect on those of us who are in there for less than an hour – think what it does to people who actually have to work there.

In December 2003, a group of Austrian shopworkers demanded compensation for being subjected to the endless Christmas soundtrack, claiming it caused them 'psychological terror'. A study found that the endless hours of Christmas carols piped into the shops made staff 'aggressive and confrontational'. (Presumably more so than would be counted as normal in Austrian supermarkets.)

Quite apart from the all-day aural attack, shopworkers over Christmas are forced to wear tinsel boas round their necks and sport endearing (i.e. stupid) Santa hats. This continues throughout the holiday period – workers in garden centres and DIY stores have to carry on gritting their teeth while armies of bleached, drained families take their annual walk through the aisles to admire the wallpaper, with no intention of buying anything.

Panic on the streets of Carlisle

If you stop to think about it, the supermarkets make you do most of their work. You have to find your own parking space, trudge to the entrance, find your own trolley, fit the coin into the slot, pull the trolley clear of all the others by using suitable force, trail round the aisles filling the trolley up while dodging the other customers, queue for ages at one of the three tills (of the sixteen available) which will be open, ram all your shopping into the flimsy carrier bags provided, pile it all up into the trolley, put your own debit card into the slot, type in your PIN, wheel your trolley back to the car, unload the shopping into the car and return your trolley, reclaiming your pound coin after a bit of shoving and coaxing. It does make you wonder what their employees do.

At Christmas, it's all much the same squared. Because you have to bear in mind this terrible, horrifying thought that will no doubt start to chill your consumerist soul some time in early December, penetrating to your very core like Jack Frost himself: *the shops are going to be closed for a whole day.*

In Germany, this happens as a matter of course at weekends. The concept of Sunday trading is one which has just never really caught on, and even on Saturdays you struggle a bit – many big towns and cities still start to wind down at lunchtime on Saturdays, except once a month when the German public are treated to a special 'long Saturday' and act as if this is a gift from God. However, if you go into the centre of any German town on a Sunday you will see a very strange sight. Even though everything is shut, the town centre will still be fairly busy.

Couples and families mill around, having come into town for the express purpose of wandering around looking in shop windows at all the things they can't buy because the shops will not be open for another 15 to 20 hours. They even have a word for this activity: it's called a *Schaufensterbummel*, literally 'an informal expedition for the purpose of gazing into shop windows'. It always was a very economical language.

20

Your Goose is Cooked

Here we go again. You will find yourself cooking a traditional Christmas dinner unless:

a) You are a vegetarian/vegan;
b) You really are intent upon declaring that you are not 'doing' it this year, and make a point of ordering a 'Good King Wenceslas' from your local Italian. (That's 'deep pan, crisp and even', by the way.)

Turkey: So here you are, just hours away from having Aunt Maud and the five kids descending on you, and you've still not defrosted the thing. Let's be honest – it's basically just a glorified chicken, isn't it? With some really odd, tough greyish-brown bits which nobody will eat. And if your local Italian restaurant, like one of my acquaintance, is offering 'turkey balls', you'd probably be wise to give that one a miss.

In 2002, a turkey race at London's famous Walthamstow dog track, known as the Gobble Cup – in which the winner would escape being served up at Christmas dinner – was called off after pressure from the RSPCA. (Presumably the participants all got eaten, then. Nice work, guys.)

Roast potatoes: Can be very nice if they are done well, although you'll find that they will be snaffled up fairly sharpish by people keen to avoid having to eat any other vegetables.

Sprouts: Best in bubble and squeak when nobody can really see what they are. Otherwise, they are a vegetable with the texture of cardboard, the appetising colour of snot and the odour of a wet dog. Who, faced with such a delicious prospect, wouldn't pile their plate high with them?

Cranberry sauce: Unless you are aiming to ward off a bout of cystitis, what exactly is the point of this? No wonder baffled foreigners think we have jam with turkey.

Bread sauce: Bread which has been made into mush. Just think carefully about what you are feeding people here. Once you have seen toddlers regurgitating porridge, you will not be able to face the stuff again for a while.

Christmas pudding: You don't expect to take your life in your hands when you sit down for dessert, but people should be made aware that Christmas pudding is possibly the most dangerous dessert ever invented. You actually have, statistically, more chance of serious injury from eating a Christmas pudding than from standing on your roof in a thunderstorm, holding your electricity aerial aloft and railing at the heavens about the injustice of God.

First of all, it's likely to be festooned with a sprig of holly – almost the sharpest and nastiest leaf known to Man. You might as well put a nettle on it and be done with it. If you manage to obtain your piece without pricking your fingers, the best is yet to come.

For it's also a dessert which people feel an unaccountable need to set on fire. (You could understand it about the sprouts, but…) Sit too close to this flaming concoction and it'll be a case of 'all I want for Christmas is my eyebrows back'.

Assuming you manage to make it through this stage of the proceedings in one piece, you then have to negotiate the minefield within. For, according to tradition, there will be small metal 'charms' buried deep within the brownish substance before you, cunningly disguised in a lake of rum sauce.

So, to summarise, this is probably the only time of year at which you will be presented with a dessert whose garnish could slice your fingers open, which could set fire to you and the dining room and which could also cause severe choking problems. And this is meant to be for pleasure.

Rum sauce and brandy butter: Do you go for one or the other? Both? Some brandy butter is absolutely horrible – it can taste like crystallised sugar and will be found, abandoned and forgotten, at the back of your fridge in early March, by which time it will have assumed the appearance and texture of a rather sorry-looking piece of Kendal Mint Cake.

Pukka Pudding

At this time of year, the celebrity recipes start to appear in the colour supplements. Saints preserve us. Yes, we all want to know how Nigella is going to baste the perfect turkey, Jamie's going to do his special Christmas pudding with rum sauce and Heston Blumenthal's going to arrange a few leaves on a plate around a selection of nut-cutlet balls in a cranberry *jus*. Do they seriously expect us to believe they are going to be cooking for the family this festive season when it's what they do for the rest of the year anyway?

Call me cynical (and if you've got this far in the book, you almost certainly have already) but I just can't see the fragrant and curvaceous Mrs Saatchi in an apron on Christmas morn, standing amid the pine needles licking a spoon while the lobster bisque boils, the turkey sizzles away in the Aga and the sprouts simmer gently on the hob. Nor can I picture young Mr Oliver skateboarding into his minimalist chrome kitchen at 7 a.m. on Christmas Day to the strains of 'God Rest Ye Merry Gentlemen', just so he can make sure those salmon filo parcels are ready for all the wacky mates he will have coming round to play charades. Let's face it, he'll be busy popping into the nearby workhouse to deliver platefuls of healthy provender to the malnourished orphans.

These people, you know, are not poor. They have to have a day off. They'll get the caterers in.

Here's a nice thought with which to end this section. In 2003, a Greenpeace report found that chemicals from the wrapping used to encase turkeys were finding their way into the meat itself. Samples of turkeys from shops across the UK contained nonylphenol, a chemical which can interfere with human DNA and affect sperm production in mammals. Quantities of phthalates – which can cause liver, kidney and testicular damage – were also detected.

Stop the Cavalry

Family, friends and more. How much worse does it get? Oh, much worse.

'I Love Christmas!'
You've got to face it – some people genuinely will. There are poor, demented souls who actually look forward to this time of year and embrace it wholeheartedly. So you'll have to have your answers ready.

'I love all the lights and things.'
Your boat really is floated by a bit of OTT illumination? You must fall over with delight when the street lamps come on. You could try switching your car's hazard warning lights on as well and standing behind it to watch the pretty orange patterns. (Don't try this on a main road.) Seriously, if you enjoy seeing your house illuminated like a tacky Las Vegas brothel then you have something lacking in your life. Maybe you were one of those people genuinely excited by that piece of 'art' which won the Turner Prize recently, which basically was an empty room with the lights going on and off.

'I love finding presents for people.'
You are the kind of person for whom the words SALE and BARGAIN evoke Pavlovian responses of joy, aren't you? The sort of consumer who can actually utter the words 'retail therapy' without any vestige of irony.

Shopping is not supposed to be an enjoyable experience. It is a seek-locate-destroy mission. You find what you want, get in there, get it and get out. If you linger or loiter, you will be distracted by the displays of luminous tubes, fake holly, Santa hats and other stuff which you really do not need. Even better – don't go out of the house for your Christmas shopping at all. Just do it all on the Internet. It was invented for the purpose of being antisocial, so let's use it for that.

'It's for the kids, really, isn't it?'
Is it? But then so is *Bear In The Big Blue House* (Channel 5, weekdays) and I challenge you to sit through that without groaning and holding your head in your hands, or without the aid of drink or medication.

'Turkey with all the trimmings is wonderful.'
Let's be honest here. Turkey is chicken with a good spin doctor. Nobody wants to eat the legs, because they are so tough and horrible, and unless you are feeding a family of twenty, you will always have platefuls of the stuff left over in the fridge. By about December 27th, it starts to look very unappetising indeed. Even to the cat.

'It only comes once a year.'
Yes, and thank God for that. Just think if you were one of those people who wished it could be Christmas every day…

'Of course, we mustn't forget the true meaning of Christmas.'
What's that, then? Making money?

'I'm looking forward to seeing all the family again.'
You're… Sorry, run that one by me again?… Nope. Still don't get it.

'There's nothing like a good get-together over Christmas.'
On the afternoon of Boxing Day, depending on your upbringing and social background, it will probably be a family tradition to decamp en masse to either a) the country lanes, for a 'hearty' walk to 'work off' that Christmas dinner, or b) the local stadium, to stand and freeze your nads off while watching the usual palaver involving twenty-two grown men fighting for possession of a ball. The way that the walk-phobic and the football-haters will counter this will be to suggest that everybody plays a board game. This is, of course, a recipe for disaster and internecine warfare, and yet people do it year after year.

22

My Husband and I

The tradition of the monarch's Christmas address to the nation was started by George V in 1932, and the Queen's first televised speech was in 1957.

Usually, the Queen delivers her homilies sitting on an armchair staring straight ahead, trying to give the impression that the kind words she has the grace to deliver to her subjects are emerging fully formed from the Royal Head, rather than being read from the Royal Autocue. It usually makes her look like an animatronic droid (perhaps designed by Bill Gates and NASA because she actually corked it back in 1998 and the government were horrified about the prospect of Charles and Camilla taking over).

Some directors, though, decide that it would be more fun to show her getting out and about a bit. The famous Richard Attenborough-directed speech was the first to do this, combining the usual armchair platitudes with a little guided tour of the stables.

These days, the sit-down footage is intercut with archive video from the last twelve months, usually of Her Majesty going about her daily business. You have to hand it to the Queen, actually – not everyone would enjoy the prospect of spending a day socialising with incontinent pensioners, foreigners, half-witted bimbos, dropouts, right-wing idiots and unqualified layabouts. But occasionally, she escapes from the family and goes out to meet the Real People.

We might see her, for example, greeting some members of the armed forces ('And what do you do? Kill people? Really? How interesting!'), some disabled children (carefully selected for their cuteness appeal and lack of obvious disfigurement), residents of rest homes ('So what do you do? Nothing? Oh, really? Neither does one!') or the few TV personalities who have managed to escape being embroiled in a sex scandal, a drugs incident or other tabloid escapade during the course of the year. It's terribly amusing to watch. You get the impression of someone being let out for the day, in order to be shown around a world which she knows nothing about, and going away equally baffled and cloistered.

The most disastrous year for Her Majesty, of course, was undoubtedly her *annus horribilis*, 1992. This was also the year in which the text was 'leaked' for the first time: well-known news comic and Scouse favourite the *Sun* published details in advance, prompting a clampdown from Buckingham Palace on making the text available to the world's press. It was suggested that reporters had obtained the recording through a BBC mole. The *Sun*'s assistant news editor at the time, the wonderfully named Leaf Kalfayan, claimed that they had done nothing wrong and had obtained the information through 'old-fashioned' techniques (whatever they may be).

It is debatable whether anybody is really so desperate to know what's going to be in the Queen's Christmas Message that they have to know *in advance*. It's not like it's the Budget or something, where some foreknowledge would help you start to plan your life around it. In fact, the only people who would really care, presumably, would be the ardent royalists – and they would be the ones most likely to consider a sneak preview to be beyond the pale.

If the BBC really wanted to make it more exciting, they could always trail it in the manner of one of their flagship dramas. First they could have some sneaky, tantalising five-second flashes of Her Maj lifting her head towards the camera – maybe shot in slow motion, in grainy primary colours – which they could start to use around October, dropping them between *Neighbours* and the News or slipping them in after *Holby City*. Then we could have the longer trailers, featuring some clips flashily edited together to the sound of Blur's 'Song 2' and ending on a dramatic voice-over: 'One country. One monarch. One message. Coming soon to BBC1.' You never know; we might just see it happen.

Here's a thought, though – she doesn't really give a toss if you have a Merry Christmas or not, you know. Let me break it to you gently – *she doesn't really know or care who you are*. She is vaguely aware of some people living in one's country who occasionally wave flags for one, and she knows that one should always wear gloves when one shakes their hand in case one catches something. The whole message thing is pre-recorded in October anyway, so you can't even get the mild frisson of hoping she might precipitate a constitutional crisis by keeling over in the middle.

Yes, the above is disrespectful to the Queen, so no doubt some *Daily Mail* readers will be foaming at the mouth and demanding for me to be sent to the Tower. Oooh, like I'm scared.

The Other Side

Since 1994, Channel 4 has broadcast an Alternative Christmas Message going head-to-head with the official one – it looks to be a tradition that will last. Hosts have included comedy rapper Ali G, US politician Reverend Jesse Jackson, actress turned animal-rights activist Brigitte Bardot, the flamboyant Quentin Crisp, impressionist Rory Bremner in the role of Princess Diana, celebrity rock wife Sharon Osbourne, *Wife Swap* star Michelle Seaborn and cartoon character Marge Simpson.

Apparently the legendary Michelle from *Wife Swap* broke down in tears on air and revealed that she had not had a Christmas present in 17 years from hubby Barry (amusingly described in the papers as an 'unemployed gambler', as if being an employed one would be a more suitable and gainful way to make a living). 'Christmas is for bloody idiots,' said Barry philosophically. In an attempt to endear himself to the hearts and minds of the nation, he added: 'It's just a load of moneymaking racket. If you buy them presents, you're giving in.'

Channel 4 seem to be scrabbling around a bit for presenters, these days. I don't think they're trying hard enough. There's a whole shedload of desperate celebrities out there. It will surely not be too long before the seasonal slot is filled by former Happy Mondays dancer and *Celebrity Big Brother* winner Bez. ('I wanna, like…wish ya…all o'ya…a fookin' Merry Christmas, right? An' it'll be fookin'…merry for me, I tell ya…when I've found me weed, like.') In case they ever run out of ideas, here are some other suggestions for high-profile names to fill the slot in future years:

- Justin from *Tikkabilla* (in Makaton sign language), with puppet friend Tamba alongside him.

- Wendy James from Transvision Vamp, who could spend the slot explaining where she has been for the last twelve years.

- Basil Brush, accompanied by with Mr Roy and Little Ticker, who ought to work in a reference to Dirty Gertie From Number Thirty somewhere.

- The legendary Tom Baker, whose contribution would be mad, but no more detached from reality than the real thing.

- Perky Geordie lass Lauren Laverne. Just because we don't see enough of her on terrestrial TV.

- Miss Hoolie from *Balamory*. Complete with arm-waving, balloon-popping, 'what's the story' effect to give us a summary of the year's events.

- An artificial intelligence based on the brain patterns of Douglas Adams.

- Claire Sweeney. Look, if she'll do *Sixty-Minute Makeover* she'll do anything.

- A genetically modified sprout. See cover.

23

Ten Good Reasons to Leave the Country at Christmas

1. You can go somewhere warmer

You don't have to spend Christmas in the UK, you know. It's not compulsory. In 2003, 1.8 million Britons fled the country over the festive period. There is nothing to stop you from absconding somewhere on a cheap package deal for the whole sorry season, even if your family throw their hands up in collective shock when you tell them you're off to Ibiza on a special 'No Hell This Noel' deal.

A spokesman for the Association of British Travel Agents – obviously an impartial observer, then – said, 'Every year there is a new record. The majority of people go away with their families. It is not a "bah, humbug" thing.' (Oh, I don't know… Have you asked them?) 'A lot of people,' went on our ABTA spokesman, 'go somewhere where there is guaranteed snow. Others go for the opposite reason, in search of the sun.'

Or maybe, Mr Travel Agent, they just go to get away from this gaudily lit, spongy, wet, miserable island with its awful Christmas music and its mindless television, where the highlight of the season for some people is that they hope they'll get to snog Angie from Human Resources under a wilting bit of poisonous plant? Had you thought of that? However, if you're still undecided, you may like to know that a leading politician once used his newspaper column to declare it 'unpatriotic' to go on holiday over the Christmas period. 'Why leave Britain when its people are at their nicest?' asked this former member of the government. Clearly, the honourable gentleman never found himself stuck in a fight between two buggy-wielding mothers for the last *Thunderbirds* toy on the shelf, or attempted to buy a cup of tea from the courteous, eloquent and clear-skinned staff at the Lakeside Thurrock Little Chef after 5 p.m. on Christmas Eve. 'For one weekend in the year,' the former Cabinet minister went on, 'even strangers will say hello to you in the street. At any other time they would be reported as suspicious characters for being so friendly.' Yes, especially around May or June every four years when they're at your door wearing coloured rosettes. Funny, that.

So, now you have a double incentive – going away at Christmas is not only unpatriotic but it will annoy the government as well. Get on that phone to the travel agent right now. Never mind listening to Her Majesty burbling on about the Commonwealth – go and visit some of it instead.

2. Only Fools and Flogging Dead Horses

The ratings war intensifies every Christmas, but some years even the BBC cannot be bothered to make an effort. You have to see the logic behind this. They know that, come 4 p.m. on Christmas Day, most people will be slumped exhausted in their chairs and will do anything to get out of playing charades or Trivial Pursuit. So they put the telly on – no matter what's on.

So you get past the inanity of the seasonal *Top of the Pops*, the grimness of the *EastEnders* special (I think it always features someone being killed or getting divorced or giving away a baby; I don't know who the hell anybody is in it but they're probably called Rickeeeee or Kazza or something) and the patronising banality of Her Majesty. Then you get the best film they could afford, usually either *Star Wars*, *The Great Escape* or something that was big in the cinemas about four years ago. And then it's on to the evening schedules.

So what do we find? A sitcom which was once funny, now reduced to endless repeats of episodes extended beyond their natural life. Is there really anyone alive who *hasn't* seen The One Where They Drop The Chandelier or The One Where Del Boy Falls Through The Bar? Same goes for *The Vicar Of Dibley*, only it wasn't as funny in the first place and so has less far to fall. We wouldn't go so far as to call TV schedulers creatively bankrupt – but when things have got so bad that they need to bring the Two Ronnies out of retirement, you do start to wonder.

3. Celebrities in festive garb

Yes, the Z-list joyfully celebrate the true meaning of the season by making themselves look ridiculous in silly hats and posing under the mistletoe, usually on the cover of *Radio Times*. We also have to endure the round of seasonal interrogations, just so we can discover what Eamonn Holmes is planning to give his mother-in-law this year, where Lorraine Kelly is buying her tree, what Nadia from *Big Brother* is planning to do on Boxing Day and how Julian Clary likes his stuffing. Why on earth do we care about this? It's all orchestrated by their agents, and always conveniently ties in to whichever seasonal extravaganza they happen to be appearing in.

4. Seasonal editions of regular TV shows

Usually a straightforward script, blown out of all proportion by the addition of some festive scenes and annoying subplots. Filmed in August, but set on Christmas Day and often featuring people having evening conversations in broad daylight while trees in full leaf can be seen behind them. Furthermore, nobody's breath mists in the air and the skies are bright blue. Who are they trying to fool?

Often, the producers decide that the best way to entertain people on Christmas Day is to take away the very elements which give a programme its individual character. And so sitcoms, for instance, are usually wrested from their everyday backdrop, the characters put on a bus or plane and forced to try and reproduce their usual chemistry in the Algarve, or Ibiza, or Miami. It rarely works.

Perhaps this would be another idea for the Queen's Christmas Message? She and Philip could present the whole thing from their sun loungers on a Spanish beach, surrounded by lobster-red English tourists in Kiss Me Quick hats and Union Jack T-shirts. At least Liz'n'Phil could be assured a vestige of patriotism and a warm welcome among the Gawd-bless-'er Benidorm set. She could raise a pina colada to us all and say how happy she was not to be spending Christmas in our dreadful country for once.

5. The Soundtrack from Hell

Taste goes out of the window as acts compete mercilessly for the Christmas number one; even otherwise sensible musicians such as the Housemartins feel the need to add bells into the mix. But I think we've covered this one.

6. Sprouts

The British housewife (or house husband) inexplicably discovers a penchant for these vegetables once a year. Your first clue to the basic *wrongness* of the sprout should be the fact that it looks so ugly. It sits there like a small, green alien being, surveying your every move as you trim the carrots and peel the potatoes. Your next should come when you cut the end off, and the hard carapace falls apart to reveal the densely packed green leaves. You should have guessed by now that eating one of these combines the enjoyment factor of school cabbage with the slight frisson of unease you get when you find a green crisp in the packet. And finally, grasping your courage in both hands, you cook it. The sprout will end up in one of two states: dense and bullet-hard, or disgustingly mushy. Furthermore, a few hours afterwards it will produce the kind of flatulence that usually takes years of practice – something combining the sound of ripping hessian with the odour of damp Labrador. Not recommended.

7. Other people's children

Unbearable at the best of times, but at Christmas you start to wonder about the case for compulsory sterilisation of some sections of the populace. Traditional seasonal sight: mother in bling and shell suit whacking wailing kid in a toyshop, punctuating her admonishment with: 'No. You. Can't. Have. A. Fuckin. PlayStation.'

8. Santa Claus

The official ones are sinister enough, and likely to make any sensible children run a mile. Why do we spend most of the year telling children never to go near funny old men, then spend most of December queuing up so that they can sit on the knee of one? Then there are the evil animatronic creatures in the shop windows, caught in their perpetual hysteresis of glee, twisting their plastic heads this way and that as they ring soundless handbells and stare sightlessly out through a haze of polystyrene snow. And then there are the seedy blokes selling 'Santa Hats' on the street. You have to ask yourself, in what other circumstances would you buy an item of dodgy headgear from a street vendor? And what, in a normal state of mind, would possess you to wear a cheap, red, felt hat topped with a white cotton-wool bobble?

9. Jesus

All right, so technically this is what it's all meant to be about. The little chap in the manger whose (allegedly virgin) mum and (probably somewhat bemused) dad couldn't get a room in the inn. The smiling infant with the halo, who didn't seem to mind being surrounded by cowpats and filthy straw. Just count yourself lucky that you don't live in America, a place where money is emblazoned with 'In God We Trust', where atheists are not considered 'true citizens' by at least one living former president (George Bush Senior, in case you were wondering) and where any attempt to question the sanity of buying your children a cross-shaped paddleball set or a 'Jesus Loves Me' sweatshirt is met with fundamentalist fury.

10. The family

Mr Colin Wood from Essex enjoyed the ultimate get-away-from-it-all Christmas break – he paid £300 for the privilege of spending the whole of one Christmas holed up in a nuclear bunker to escape the fallout from his atomic family. Colin had a copy of *A Christmas Carol* to read and was issued with supplies of spam, beans, water and government-issue toilet roll. Reportedly, he had more fun than anybody spending Christmas back home in Basildon.

24

No! Not the Yuletide Round-up!

Yes, this is the one chance people get to communicate with people they haven't seen in years – and who actually don't remember (and don't care) if they are alive or dead.

The Christmas circular is a remarkable thing. Nearly always written in the third person, it is an uneasy mix of self-congratulation and self-flagellation. It's a competitive summary of the family's events of the year, often interspersed with incongruous references to the events of the day. Some people call it 'Boast By Post' – but that doesn't quite encompass the darker side of the Christmas round robin, in which every misfortune to have happened to the sender over the past twelve months is depicted in searing detail.

One couple of my acquaintance despairs at the annual 20-page update from a family they met once, briefly, on a camping holiday in Norfolk. Other friends receive an annual update which, for the past five years, has been sent to the previous owners of the house; they do not seem to take the lack of a reply as a hint. I also know of one gleeful mailing entitled 'Just For Yule', which in recent years has taken to signing off with: 'You'd better send me your news or you won't get "Just For Yule" next year!' As threats go, it's not the most effective.

In recent years, senders have started to realise the potential of satire, and the missives have started to take on a vestige of irony. The best Christmas circulars, though, should be remarkably unselfconscious and should offer the most harmonious balance of shameless vaunting, pointless trivia and forensic details of family illness.

Email, sadly, has just made this sort of thing easier: 20-page attachments detailing the holidays in the Lake District of the family of someone you briefly worked with six years ago are just what you want clogging up your mailbox. Some of them – the horror – even have interactive footnotes and hyperlinks. It won't be long before they offer webcam-links to live, interactive coverage of Uncle Bert's prostate operation and the solemn inhuming of Tiddles.

The sad thing is that you actually start to look forward to them. You find yourself wondering who will have produced the best interactive flow diagram, photostory or 30-page epic this year. You start to take bets. Will Jenny and Patrick from Edinburgh win the 'best illustrative effect' award again with their border of alternating miniature Christmas trees and sprigs of holly? Or will Neil and Natasha in Ashby de la Zouch trounce them this year with their watermarks of grinning snowmen?

And should you fail to receive one from a regular Christmas correspondent, you will start to wonder, with a pang of near-longing, where it is. You'll almost miss the tales of the over-achieving offspring who were still in short trousers when you last met them and the distant relatives whose gender is not clear from their name (Bufty, Biddy, Ninky). You'll hanker after the forensic detailing of every medical crisis suffered by the correspondent's aged aunt/mother/tabby cat.

Anyway, to aid you in your quest to produce your annual Christmas circular for the entertainment of your family and friends, here is a template to be followed:

The Old Rectory
Little Cobbling
Barsetshire

15th December 20**

Friends!

Well! Doesn't time fly??! Another year gone by, and here we are. *Tempus fugit*, as they say in Latin; and how appropriate, for how very like the fall of Ancient Rome our family life has been this year with all its comings and goings. That's not to say that the family are Barbarians!!! (Although at times we have wondered about Uncle Jonty!!!)

This year began with our attempts to fit laminate flooring in the new extension. What a palaver! Michael had to have several attempts to get it right, but in the end he managed to win the battle, and with only a small injury. Thankfully his visit to Outpatients did not detract from our enjoyment of the splendid new floor (although the application of Didi-7 has as yet proven ineffective at getting the bloodstains out).

Maud, following her investigative surgery, seems to have perked up a little – a surprise, as we had believed her to be not long for this world. She has moved into the new spare room above the extension and is proving to be an endless source of entertainment with her wartime anecdotes and requests for warm leek broth.

Sadly, the Grim Reaper stalks through all our lives, and this year he took Great-Aunt Alice from us after a difficult year involving much hoisting, drip-feeding and draining of boils. Her 'natural' burial in open woodland may not have been to everyone's taste but it was stipulated in the will, and I'm sure the tree marked with her name will come to be a solace to hikers and casual passers-by alike. We have put the mahogany drop-leaf table in her room instead.

We also lost Consuela, the au pair, although in happier circumstances. She was in many ways a trying young woman. Thankfully the shade of Eggshell Blue with which Michael has painted her old room has almost covered up the mural of Marilyn Manson; one would barely know it was there in a dim light.

Charmian passed all of her A-levels with flying colours and still found time to take the euphonium to Grade Seven (the reverberation of her practice around the house has come to have a comforting, homely feel to it) and also to lead the Under-18 Hockey team to the semi-finals of the Inter-Schools Championship – although their progress to the final was impeded by some dubious tactics from the opposition. That unfortunate business from last year appears to have blown over, and thankfully Charmian only has two more appointments with the school psychologist before it can be laid to rest for good.

Raphael continues to be the star of the Upper Fourth, and endears himself to all with his hilarious impressions of all the teachers. Inigo, meanwhile, is frightfully artistic and loves to express himself in all available media; the kitchen wall still bears testament to his fabulously inventive Jackson Pollock period this summer.

Uncle Hector is doing well, or so I believe, and is making the most of his limited resources. The food, I am told, is good, and he has made a few new friends. Circumstances, sadly, prevent us from visiting as often as we would like, but I understand his application for parole is being considered.

Some clarification is needed following last year's letter in which I stated that we had 'lost' Timmy. Many thanks to those of you who sent in your sympathy cards, including those who believed that Timmy was an aged uncle or a young child, and not, in fact, our Golden Retriever. I should make clear that he merely went missing, and did actually return on New Year's Day with a hungry look in his eye. It may have been this which led to his downfall, as this year he was in fact knocked over by a milk float and subsequently had to be put down.

The tiling in the bathroom, detailed in last year's letter, is now complete. The pattern is perhaps a little more abstract than one would have liked, and there is an interesting 'modern art' effect in one corner indicating the point at which Michael temporarily lost control of both his temper and the tiling knife. Thankfully, the course of medication was successful and he has been able to undertake a number of successful DIY projects since.

Felicity has continued with her challenging and rewarding church works. The poor can be so interesting when you start talking to them; such *colourful* lives!! She has also progressed well with her Open College Network Level 3 in Non-Verbal Counselling Processes and her distance studies of Aura Therapy. She hopes to become fully qualified for next year.

We wish you all a pleasant and prosperous New Year.

Yours, in seasonal joy,
Felicity, Michael, Charmian, Raphael and Inigo,
and of course Bunty the cockatoo.

25

Where's Your Career? It's Behind You!

It's the pantomime season again. Every pantomime has to include at least some of the following:

Desperate/faded soap actor

Usually playing Buttons, or equivalent. On the poster, it will say KEVIN SPROCKET in large letters, underneath a picture of his gurning mug – and below, in smaller letters, as if conceding that there will be a section of the populace which has never felt the need to keep up with the antics of soaps, 'Bertie MacKenzie from TV's *Shadwell Square*.' This will probably leave you none the wiser, especially if your only experience of the plotlines comes from the brief trailers you occasionally catch by accident, plus a horrified fascination with the Alison Graham column in the *Radio Times* just to remind yourself how fortunate you are that you never have to endure this shit.

So all the time he's prancing round on the stage making double entendres, throwing sweets out at the audience and mooning hopelessly after Cinderella/Snow White/whoever, you'll be distracted. You'll be trying to remember if he is the one who got his wife's sister pregnant, the one who decided he was gay and had an affair with his teacher, or the one who lost his memory after being hit by a car driven by his vengeful ex-wife and ended up marrying his stepdaughter's best friend.

Reality TV 'star'

The above applies, only about five times more horrific. You do wonder what's happening in the world when the Fairy

Godmother in *Snow White* is played by Gobby Letitia from *The Scouse House*, the title role in *Cinderella* is taken by Fit Kayleigh from *Desperate Students* and the Genie in *Aladdin* is that fat bloke who was the first to be evicted from *Shagfest Island* and who you thought would never work again after that incident with Wincey Willis and the bicycle pump.

You actually have to hand it to the media industry – it got fed up waiting around for genuine stars to come through and so it generated its own. People who, just a few short months ago, were that annoying twit in the corner of your office who kept telling everyone they were going to be famous are now Z-list celebs with a whole career of pantomimes, 'personal appearances', rubbish records and *Heat* magazine spreads ahead of them. You have to ask yourself why it took so long for them to think of it, frankly.

Dodgy scenery
This is not a blockbuster movie. Even the best stage sets for pantomimes are not that convincing. They spend all the money on one big castle/courtyard set and the rest is usually painted backdrops of forests and the like. These prove very useful – the double act will have a bit of 'amusing' banter in front of them while the scene is changed for the final big number.

Kids called up on stage
You sometimes wonder if this is how it's taught at Panto School, because it's always the same. Four cute children, interviewed by the comic turn, who is desperately hoping he doesn't make one of them burst into tears. Always ends with smallest and cutest apparently not getting a prize, and then going home laden down with a goodie-bag bigger than they are.

Huge song-and-dance number
With lots of leg, 'for the dads'. Here is where you'll find the 20-year-olds who are hungry, the Gemmas and Charlottes and

Lucys who hope to be in the West End this time next year, or at the very least getting a line or two in *The Bill*.

Old-fashioned values

Good triumphs over Evil and, indeed, Evil is revealed to be a bit half-hearted about the whole thing at the end, the villainess usually having her wicked nature purged by the simple application of a spell or even just by deciding that she can't be bothered with all this cackling and wearing black velvet any more. Despite the ministrations of political correctness elsewhere in the world, it's good to know that there are some places where the boy will always get the girl, endings are happy and the status quo is resolved. This is despite the attempts of certain London boroughs to make people enamoured of more 'progressive' pantomimes where Snow White empowers the Seven Persons of Restricted Growth to campaign for better labourers' rights in the mine, Cinderella explores her repressed lesbian feelings for her stepmother and Jack and the Giant sit down and talk out their differences before warning of the hazards of genetically modified beanstalk crops.

26

It's a Terrible Life

That extra-thick copy of the *Radio Times* is about to thud on to your doormat, and you're ready to go through it with the highlighter pen to decide which of the veritable cornucopia of cinematic delights you will be sampling this Yuletide. It's very likely that you will encounter most, if not all, of the following.

The Wizard of Oz

The one everyone should see. Once. If you are a serious film buff or a Friend of Dorothy, then repeated viewings can be excused, but otherwise they are not recommended – especially in the light of the ending. **Lowdown:** Technicolor extravaganza about a girl and her dog who, after rather clumsily landing their airborne house on top of a witch with stripy socks, skip merrily along a yellow brick road and gather a crack team of mercenaries together to visit the Wonderful Wizard. These include a lion with no courage, a tin man with no heart and a straw man with no brain (who still somehow manages to get up and walk). **Best bit:** They discover that the genius of the Emerald City is really no more than a little man who overcompensates for his insecurities with a Hammond organ and a better light show than Jean Michel Jarre. It's all an endearing little fantasy, until... **Worst bit:** When Dorothy wakes up and it's all been a dream. I mean, as they say, WTF?! 'And then I woke up and it was all a dream' is the lamest line in fiction, reproduced by Year 7 pupils up and down the land in a vain attempt to provide a 'twist' to their flights of fancy. And here it is in one of the most popular films of all time. The crap ending to beat all crap endings. **Spoiler:** They *were* in Kansas all along.

The Great Escape

The one that never goes away. **Lowdown:** Star-studded cast's attempt to break out of a German prisoner-of-war camp, despite such potentially challenging handicaps as a claustrophobic tunnel-digger (Charles Bronson) and a blind forger (Donald Pleasence). **Best bits:** When Gordon Jackson gets caught out by the German who says 'Have a good day', and, of course, that motorbike ride by Steve McQueen up and down the barbed wire. Every time you watch, you're convinced that, one day, he's actually going to do it. **Worst bit:** Comedy German accents. **Spoiler:** James Garner survives.

Star Wars

Lowdown: A glorified Western in space. Ingrained into the psyche of every thirtysomething in the land, all of whom desperately try to convince themselves that they are going to enjoy it as much as they did when they were seven (and who try to block the words 'Menace' and 'Phantom' out of their memory). **Best bit:** Many to choose from, but 'These are not the droids you are looking for' is a contender. Plus Han Solo's 'stupid conversation anyway'. **Worst bit:** The picaresque plot is ricepaper-thin. And the end battle sequence in the Death Star goes on and on. **Spoiler:** Darth Vader is Luke's father. (Oh, come on, you're not saying you didn't know *that*?)

The Sound of Music

Lowdown: The everyday tale of a governess, their father, some nuns and seven terrifying Aryan children trained with military precision, all of whom occasionally burst into song for no readily apparent reason. **Best bits:** 'Are Daddy and Uncle Max going to push the car all the way to Switzerland?' and 'Reverend Mother

– I have sinned', when the nuns who have sabotaged the Nazis' car hold out the components with penitent expressions on their faces. **Worst bit:** When, in the middle of a conversation, the Reverend Mother stands by the window and breaks into 'Climb Every Mountain'. Perhaps I'm just not a show tunes kind of guy. **Spoiler:** They win the singing contest. And escape. (Look, you're not seriously expecting them to get lined up and shot by the Nazis, are you?)

The Family Man
A more recent entry into the canon, but one which, because of its strong seasonal flavour, is bound to pop up year after year. **Lowdown:** The millennial take on *It's A Wonderful Life*. Driven executive Jack Campbell (Nicolas Cage) prevents a hold-up in a store and, as a reward from a 'guardian angel', is given a 'glimpse' of a whole new life with a wife and family in the suburbs. The said guardian angel (in a natty sports car) explains the plot to him in enigmatic fits and starts. It's the life he could have had, if he'd married his girlfriend (Téa Leoni) instead of pursuing the American Dream of making lots of money. **Best bit:** Cage's bemusement as he gradually adjusts to his new environment. **Worst bit:** The having-it-all ending, which makes little sense. Where do the kids go? **Spoiler:** They get it together. (Like, duh, you didn't see that coming.)

Die Hard
Yes, it's Christmas in this film, in case you hadn't noticed. **Lowdown:** Hilariously over-the-top thriller in which every member of the cast is always a millisecond away from cracking up into paroxysms of laughter. A post-*Moonlighting* Bruce Willis single-handedly takes on a whole tower block full of terrorists, led by the chilling Hans Gruber (Alan Rickman), who is probably not related to either Lieutenant Gruber from *'Allo 'Allo* or Mr Gruber from the Paddington books. Many of the muscled

Teutonic stooges, it should be noted, sport the haircuts of German soft-rockers *circa* 1990. Everybody has those incredible self-reloading machine pistols, and nobody can shoot straight except when the plot demands it. **Best bit:** Either Willis's piece of hosepipe-aided abseiling, or the sudden revelation of the two guns taped to his back in the climax – it's the point at which the film finally tips over into self-parody, and it's great. **Spoiler:** The terrorists are actually glorified bank robbers. And Hans corks it.

The Snowman

Lowdown: A simple tale of a boy and his snowman who comes to life. And that's it, really. To be found on Channel 4, every single year for the past twenty-odd years and no doubt for time immemorial. **Best bit:** everybody's just waiting for the 'Walking In The Air' sequence. **Spoiler:** He melts.

Jingle All the Way

Lowdown: It's Arnie Goes Shopping. Schwarzenegger plays a father who, to make up for being late for his son's karate class, promises to get him this year's must-have toy, 'Turbo-Man', for Christmas. From such a thin premise comes a deeply dull film. And, disappointingly, Arnie doesn't storm through the shops in shades and leather jacket, proclaiming, 'Uzi nine-millimeee-ter, geev mee de tooy, ass-hole-eee.' No, it's Arnold playing an all-American dad and playing it for laughs. **Worst bit:** The opportunity to satirise Christmas commercialism is totally missed.

The Railway Children

Lowdown: Sequence of picaresque adventures in the life of a middle-class Edwardian family whose father is arrested on a trumped-up charge and thrown into jail. Rather than relocating to the slums of the inner cities, they are so poor that they have to get the train up to the wilds of Yorkshire – where all they can afford is that traditional haven of the destitute, a rambling country cottage with a huge garden and roses over the door. Even more implausibly, Mother is supporting the entire family with that well-known money-spinner, writing short stories for magazines (longhand, and in the freezing cold), when in real life she'd probably have gone on the game. Hilarious and entertaining consequences ensue, featuring such unlikely elements as a lost Russian, a landslide on the track, an injured boy in the tunnel, a puppet show and a misunderstanding over a birthday. The eponymous railway plays a large part in the proceedings, and as such the film is not exactly renowned as a Public Information film about the dangers of playing on train-tracks. And it's one for dads everywhere, as it features Jenny Agutter in her jailbait incarnation (while the recent remake capitalises on her newfound status as MILF). **Best bit:** Some contend it's the landslide and the sequence where they frantically wave their red petticoats at the train. But most would say it's 'Daddy, my Daddy!' **Worst bit:** The way you get the feeling that a lot of the interludes are just marking time until the end. **Spoiler:** Daddy's released.

The James Bond Film

Impossible to say which one it will be. Just hope for a *Thunderball* or a *GoldenEye* rather than a *Licence To Kill* or an *Octopussy*. **Lowdown:** Middle-aged spy and lothario, code-named 007, shags and shoots his way round a variety of exotic locations, dispatching henchmen, uncovering international conspiracies and making deadpan quips. The girl he shags first in the film is always murdered by the villain's henchmen. Bond then acquires a main squeeze, who is usually called something like Honey Lovetunnel or Tiffany Goodhead. About two-thirds of the way into the film, he and the lady – a lissom creature clad in little but a bikini (for the purposes of the plot, naturally) – inveigle their way into the villain's headquarters, which is usually a vast arena hidden inside a volcano, underwater base or space station. Villain proceeds to reveal his entire plot to our hero, saying, 'the information will be no use to you, Mr Bond, as you will shortly die.' Rumbustious climax ensues, with lots of explosions and shooting. Bond and lissom lady escape in lifeboat, dinghy, space shuttle, et cetera and engage in a bit of nookie while the credits roll. It's nice work if you can get it. **Best bit:** Some kind of innuendo, like the 'attempting re-entry' line from *Moonraker*. Or one of the spectacular chase scenes, when that familiar bass-line kicks in. **Worst bit:** Usually the acting, which always comes from the 'stick it in a sandwich and spread it with mustard' school of subtlety. **Spoiler:** James Bond always wins. Except in the George Lazenby outing, *On Her Majesty's Secret Service*, where the villains manage to bump off his new bride.

27

No Room at the Inn

If you have small children, you will at some point be forced to endure the most excruciating of theatrical performances.

Here is where you will see Pushy Parents in the raw. The spirit of goodwill is, again, non-existent here. Their instincts honed by years of cajoling and hustling for the best nurseries and the best school catchment places, they will have exercised their cut-throat skills to the extreme in order to secure the best roles for their little darlings. The parents of Mary, Joseph, the Three Kings and the Shepherds will be looking pretty smug. Those whose tiny thespians have been relegated to Second Angel – or worse, Oxen – will be the ones scowling at the back, their arms folded, muttering about what a mistake it is to give such an important role to someone like Jamie who is basically illiterate and has behaviour problems, when Harry knows the role of Joseph by heart as he played it in nursery last year, and if they'd only thought before putting the reputation of the school at risk, and this is going to make them reconsider their place on the PTA.

You should not expect the acting standards to be as high as in the version of *The Merry Wives of Windsor* you saw at Stratford the other week. And the special effects employed are not going to be giving The Mill (purveyors of exploding spaceships for *Doctor Who*) any sleepless nights. On the other hand, you won't have any trouble spotting the future talent. Especially if you're standing next to his mother, who will dig you in the ribs with her bony elbow and announce in a stage whisper, 'That's my Liam!'

One of the perennial problems of the Nativity is that it requires the inclusion of livestock. Several productions I have seen have, rather wisely, taken the cop-out option of relying on stuffed toys and a large bucketload of imagination. The nativity-play director who decides to employ a genuine donkey is brave indeed, and has obviously never seen the famous episode of *Blue Peter* with the loose-bowelled elephant.

If you want to do something as seemingly innocent as bringing your video-camera along, you'll need to check – paranoia about nefarious recording of children is at an all-time high. The authorities are no doubt terrified that you'll capture for ever that moment when little Shane whacks little Callum in the face with his shepherd's crook and that you'll get 200 quid for sending it in to *Don't Children Do The Stupidest Things?* or *You Gotta Laugh, Ain't Ya?* or any of those other TV *schadenfreude* spectaculars.

The best way to bring the nativity play to a quick close

Some years ago, a well-meaning infant-school teacher of my acquaintance decided that the best way to deal with the most disruptive boy in her class was to give him some responsibility. First of all, she got him sharpening pencils and giving out books, and she was pleased to notice an appreciable turn for the better in his behaviour.

One day, she sat him down and told him the good news – because he had been so well behaved over the past few weeks, he was going to be allowed to take part in the school's nativity play. Moreover, he was going to play the very important role of the innkeeper in Bethlehem.

'But I want to know that you won't let us down,' the teacher said sternly. 'You have to be a very, very good boy and a very helpful boy if you're going to do this.' The reformed thug promised that he would.

The day of the nativity play came and the school hall was packed with parents. Mary and Joseph shuffled on, accompanied by an unconvincing donkey on wheels, and Mary giggled as she saw her mummy in the audience.

Joseph cleared his throat. 'Innkeeper!' he declaimed. 'My wife and I have come to be taxed. Do you have a room where we might stay the night?'

And the young innkeeper, remembering his promise to be good and helpful, jumped up and, ushering them forward delightedly, shouted:

'Yes! We've got lots of rooms! Come in, come in!'

It's got to be worth a go.

28

Blue Christmas

Or alternatively: Tonight, thank God it's them instead of you.

The relentless pressure to have a Good Time at Christmas is in stark contrast to the actual misery of the season for a great many people. Here are just a few examples:

- After a three-day storm on **Mount Everest** in 1997, six Tibetans, five of them children, died in attempts to escape the severe snowstorms on the Himalayan passes, according to survivors who reached Kathmandu.

- At Christmas 1963, a **train crash** in Szolnok, Hungary caused the deaths of 45 people. The driver of one of the trains was found guilty and was sent to prison for 11 years. And in **December 1906**, 22 people died when an express train ran into the back of another during a blizzard at Elliot Junction in Scotland.

- In 2002, winter hit the **Czech Republic** hard and the freezing weather resulted in several deaths among the country's homeless. Shelters became overcrowded and had difficulty responding to the increased demand.

- Not so very merry either for the following **famous dead people**, all of whom popped up to see the angels (or down to meet with the others) on Christmas Day itself: Pope

Adrian the First in 795, Japanese Emperor Yoshihito in 1926, comedian WC Fields in 1946, film legend Charlie Chaplin in 1977, Romanian dictator Nikolai Ceausescu in 1989 and actor Dean Martin in 1995. (On the other hand, the parents of singers Dido, Annie Lennox, Shane MacGowan and Little Richard, DJ Kenny Everett, actor Humphrey Bogart, actress Sissy Spacek, model Helena Christensen and mathematical clever-clogs Sir Isaac Newton all received a festive little bundle of joy – as all of the above celebs share their birthdays with the baby Jesus. Aaah.)

- The **suicide rate** is higher at Christmas than at any other time of the year. This is partly because people imagine others having a wonderful time in the bosom of their nuclear family and that they are the only ones being miserable. The Samaritans advise – and this is absolutely true – that you should not feel obliged to enjoy Christmas. This seems like excellent advice. As long as you remember that most people will be having a fairly crap time as well, you can't go wrong. One should also add that the Samaritans also advise you not to bottle up your emotions and to talk to someone. This should, presumably, be someone other than Father Christmas.

- **Cyclone Tracy** hit Darwin, Australia over Christmas 1974. Forty-nine people were killed in Darwin itself, while a further 16 lives were lost at sea. Approximately 650 people were treated for injuries on Christmas Day, while more than 35,000 people were evacuated in the days that followed. Power, water, sanitation and communications were lost and over 80 per cent of all buildings were destroyed.

- And, taking us back to a smaller, human level, the story of **Los Angeles woman Linda Sartor** should be a salutary tale to all who are overkeen on their Christmas decorations. For a start, she began decorating her house around Hallowe'en every year. And yes, she was one of those people who delighted in displaying an array of evil grinning snowmen and no less than four artificial trees in various rooms throughout her house – as well as lights on seven trees outside. Unfortunately, Linda overloaded the lights and the electrical short-circuit set fire to her trees, burning her house down. Firefighters arrived promptly and had the blaze under control in a matter of minutes, but this was not enough to save Linda, who was burned to death.

Seasonal philosophy

Someone who thought he had a handle on all this death and disaster was Aleksandr Solzhenitsyn, the Russian-born Nobel Prize winner for literature (1970), who said, 'Over half a century ago while I was still a child, I recall hearing a number of older people offer the following explanation for the great disasters that had befallen Russia: "Men have forgotten God, that's why all this has happened."'

Rrrright. Thanks, Alex. It didn't, perhaps, occur to you that the old codgers were saying that because they were old and miserable and wanted something to moan about, and that whingeing about the laxness and moral turpitude of the younger generation is just what old people *do*? This sort of thing is, I'm afraid, often quoted by those who want to see September 11th and the 2004 Asian tsunami as 'wake-up calls from God', things that happened because millions have ignored or forsaken their deity at Christmas. Jolly nice of the all-seeing, all-knowing, all-powerful God to do this just because people aren't remembering his birthday, I must say. I don't know about you, but if having thousands of people obliterated in horrific disasters is what a nice God does, I'd hate to see a horrible one.

29

In the Grotto

t's that man again. In the words of mulleted middle-of-the-road American songster Richard Marx, wherever you go, whatever you do, he'll be right there waiting for you. From about mid-November onwards, you just can't escape him. He's on everything from adverts to wrapping paper, from magazines to shop-window displays.

Don't forget the live ones. Around this time of year, struggling portly actors suddenly find themselves back in demand – first of all there's the possibility of a Widow Twankey at the local theatre (or failing that, at least the back end of a large and unconvincing cow) and then there's all the Santas. If you have children, this is the time at which you have to start making up all kinds of excuses as to why there are so many of them. You could just say that he's got lost, I suppose, and that as a bloke he's never going to stop and ask for directions. (Mind you, what kind of man is happy to trot around in red velour trimmed with white fur? Hmm.)

And so we have the plethora of Grottos. No shopping centre or department store seems to be complete without one, more's the pity. They are usually no more than a corner of a room covered with a bit of white Jabolite and a few fake icicles, with, if you're really unlucky, some Christmassy music playing in the background. You then have to queue for three hours (losing your place if your child needs the toilet) just for the privilege of five minutes with a scary man in a beard who will give your offspring carte blanche to say what they really want for Christmas and thereby embarrass you into buying it.

Things don't always go according to plan, of course. Santas are only human, and sometimes their failings lead to situations which nobody could have foreseen. Take a look at a few of these stories:

- A hired Santa Claus at a shopping centre in New Zealand was apparently **scaring children** by saying 'Ho ho ho!' with a little too much gusto. After a number of children emerged from Santa's Grotto in tears, managers advised new Santas to turn down the volume of the jollity a little.

- A Norfolk Santa was sacked in 2004 for having **'the wrong attitude'**. Philip 'Peachy' Mead, 66, was asked to leave the Norwich John Lewis store after store managers said he had 'not met their expectations'. Regional Equity secretary Mr Mead – who had previously worked as a holiday camp Redcoat and had been working with children since 1961 – had asked for a throne to sit on so that he didn't tower menacingly over the children. When his request was turned down, he reportedly became angry.

- In a Llanelli shopping centre, staff are using a **live camera** to monitor Santa's consultations – allegedly to protect him from allegations of child abuse. 'It's just to give parents peace of mind,' says manager Gilmour Jones, who adds that most parents are supportive of the move. Of course, litigious children can also use the footage as evidence when they don't get the PlayStation or iPod they have asked for.

- And also in Llanelli, **cabbie Tony James** – who traditionally dressed up as Santa while working to cheer up his customers – was told by the council that he had to lose the disguise as he would not look like the photo on his ID badge. Presumably there was also something of a conflict of interests – you don't expect Santa to put two quid on the sleigh meter before you even get in.

Meanwhile, church leaders in York took issue with the Christmas display in **Satan's Grotto** (*sic*) at the York Dungeon. Visitors were greeted by a man dressed as the Devil sporting a red face and horns, while gifts such as severed fingers were handed out. The attraction also included elves impaled on spikes, robins roasting over an open fire and Santa being put in a witch's cauldron and boiled. A Dungeon spokesman said the display was 'not to be taken too seriously'. Visitor Barney Smithers, 43, said, 'Nothing unusual about a bit of torture, mayhem and violence at Christmas.' He added, 'And if we get bored with having the in-laws round we can always go to the York Dungeon for some light relief.'

And finally, if you want to see true madness, go to www.santarchy.com where you will find all kinds of Santa shenanigans. Not for the faint-hearted.

30

I'm a Celebrity – I'll Get Me Coat

Celebrities – what are they? In this day and age, it's becoming increasingly apparent that they are simply ordinary people who got lucky. They may bang on about their hard work and talent, but then there are an awful lot of hard-working, talented people out there without their own prime-time TV shows.

In recent years, it's become possible to short-circuit the whole tedious process of playing gigs to six people at the Pig and Whistle and appearing at 3 a.m. for a cough and a spit with a patronising presenter on Radio TinPot who's never heard of you. This is celebrity for the I Want It Now generation. You know – all those annoying twentysomethings with their pierced lips and their retro mullets, grasping their 2.2s in Batik With Showbiz Studies from the University of Central Rutland, moaning that they 'can't get on the housing ladder' when what they mean is that they can't move straight away into a three-bed semi with a big drive and a garden in the most desirable part of town and that they might have to slum it for a bit. Diddums. The celeb system is just what they're after – they can leapfrog all the usual boring stuff like hard work and go straight for the international acclaim and the personal stylist. For the obligatory fifteen minutes.

This is why we experience a thrill of *schadenfreude* when it doesn't work out. That 18-year-old novelist given a ridiculous advance, whose book sank without trace when people started to realise it was a load of tripe. The *Pop Idol* winner who was vanished back into obscurity and the *Big Brother* contestants who, for ten weeks, were famous enough to be known by first name only and are now lost, like tears in the rain. (Whither Sada? Nicola? Spencer? Marco? And who, indeed, gives a festering pile of horseshit?) And don't forget the deliciously salutary tale of One True Voice, the TV-manufactured boy band who predicted on *Richard And Judy* that their career would last ten years, and who were only out by nine years and ten months.

At Christmas – to get back to the point of our book – we may superficially wish joy to the world and goodwill to all men. But if you've already read this far, you'll have realised that this isn't generally very much fun, and that it can be much more enjoyable simply to take the piss.

And when things go wrong for celebrities over the festive season, you start to wonder why there hasn't already been a cable documentary on this very subject.

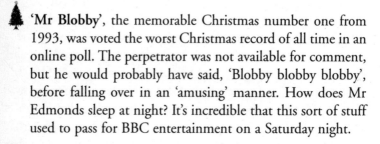

'**Mr Blobby**', the memorable Christmas number one from 1993, was voted the worst Christmas record of all time in an online poll. The perpetrator was not available for comment, but he would probably have said, 'Blobby blobby blobby', before falling over in an 'amusing' manner. How does Mr Edmonds sleep at night? It's incredible that this sort of stuff used to pass for BBC entertainment on a Saturday night.

Jack Nicholson admitted in an interview that his parents would often put a lump of coal in his Christmas stocking if he had been naughty. 'I don't know what getting that coal did to me,' admitted Jack. 'I know what it did to me then! It destroyed me. I think my parents knew they'd overplayed their hand.' Still, I'm sure the millions he now commands for roles are something of a comfort.

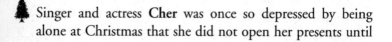

Singer and actress **Cher** was once so depressed by being alone at Christmas that she did not open her presents until

July. Let's hope her seasonal gift selection didn't include a basket of fresh fruit.

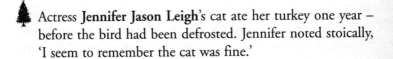 Actress **Jennifer Jason Leigh**'s cat ate her turkey one year – before the bird had been defrosted. Jennifer noted stoically, 'I seem to remember the cat was fine.'

Robert Downey Jr won't ever dress up as Father Christmas again after he turned up drunk one year and frightened the children. 'People were really scared!' said the actor. 'The children were like, "Why is Santa so on edge? Why is he drunk?"' The children were told he had been in the chimney for three weeks.

Peter Fonda bought presents for his mother the year after she had died and insisted on putting them under the tree. He then made the rest of the family swear on the Bible that he was now head of the household.

One Christmas, **Peter Criss**, drummer with the band Kiss, had a few drinks and ended up firing a pistol at the Christmas tree – because his wife had refused to let him be the one who put the star on top.

Halle Berry's worst Christmas experience was when she saw her mother eating the cookies from the plate they had put out for Santa Claus. 'I never let her forget it!' Halle said grimly.

Friends star **Matt Le Blanc** admits to a seasonal transgression: he used to peel the sellotape off the presents, pull the toy out to have a sneaky play with it, then put everything back in the box, seal it all up again and put it back under the tree. It was only recently that he admitted this to his mother. Of course, it's entirely possible that he made this unlikely story up to enliven a dull interview.

'Everyone, have a great time. But get pissed at home.' That was celebrity chef **Keith Floyd**'s exhortation to the nation after he received a 32-month driving ban for being three times over the legal alcohol limit. Floyd added that the police who arrested him were 'very courteous'. That was a bit remiss of them.

Catherine Zeta Jones supposedly likes nothing better than a festive game of bingo on Boxing Day. 'It's something Catherine has done since she was a little girl growing up in Wales,' says a supposed 'insider'. 'She used to make all the balls with numbers on them, the cards and organise the prizes and she still plays now, only she probably doesn't have to make it. Michael thinks it's a bizarre game, especially all that bingo lingo, but it's a bit of fun and last year he won a nice bottle of aftershave.' A lot of balls, however you look at it.

Actress **Rhona Mitra** experienced 'tree guilt' when shopping for festive foliage. 'I drove by this place and there were all these trees and I felt like I needed to stop and get one and I went in and I felt like I was in a dog shelter. I felt really bad for the trees that were being left behind. I thought "Oh my God, look at you, you don't have a head – maybe you should come back with me, as well as the lovely chubby, fat bushy tree that I got…"'

However, these days you don't need to be a film star to be rated a 'celebrity'. The entire industry of magazines like *Heat* survives on the self-perpetuating, tail-eating idea of the 'famous for fifteen minutes' mini-celeb – and our next section has a little look at what they will be doing this year.

31

It's the Best Celebrity Christmas Ever

For those lamenting a lack of celeb-based reality TV in the Christmas line-up, we present some of the seasonal ideas which have been thrown across the table at planning meetings recently. And as ITV's unfortunate schedulers are still utterly desperate to find something to combat the Christmas special of *Doctor Who* (yaaaay!) they may yet be taken up.

Star Santas
In which well-known salad-dodgers Michael Winner, Christopher Biggins, Johnny Vegas and Rik Waller are each given a grotto and a sack of presents, plus some brief tuition in basic ho-ho-hoing and verbal abuse of reindeer. They are then dressed in Santa costumes and unleashed in the Trafford Centre, Sheffield's Meadowhall, Lakeside at Thurrock and London's Oxford Street respectively. Hidden cameras monitor their progress in the grottos, and points are deducted for scaring children. First prize – a night on the town with Rebecca Loos. Second prize – two nights on the town with Rebecca Loos. Boom-boom.

Celebrity Christmas Building Site
Ten hapless celebrities – including Abi Titmuss, Tony Mortimer and Les Dennis – are made to don hard hats and sling hods over their shoulders in order to construct a Barratt Home within ten days for a family to move into on Christmas Day. If they make it on time, the celebs get to have a glass of sherry round the fire with the lucky family, and if they don't, then they get gunged by Ant'n'Dec. Hosted by Gordon 'Krypton Factor' Burns.

Strictly Christmas Gardening

Ten D-list celebrities are forced to take up their trowels and shears and turn a 20-acre wasteland into an award-winning show garden, complete with water feature, pergola and laburnum arch, in time for the National Gardens Championship – or face the wrath of Alan 'bonny' Titchmarsh, Charlie 'look at my charlies' Dimmock and Diarmuid 'incomprehensible' Gavin. Hosted by the lovely Sarah Raven, with voice-over by Sean Pertwee. Obviously filmed in the summer, but we can get away with it.

Ultimate Celebrity Carol-Singing

Featuring Jenny Powell, That Bloke Married to Jade Goody, Annabel Croft, Timmy Mallett, The Lovely Debbie McGee, Michael Barrymore and Elton John's Partner David Furnish. They have two days to learn perfectly the harmonies to 'Ding Dong Merrily On High', 'Once in Royal David's City' and 'We Wish You a Merry Christmas', before being divided into two teams and unleashed on the streets of Ashby de la Zouch on Christmas Eve to see who can raise the most money and accrue the fewest insults. All for charidee, obviously. (I'm already starting to get a nasty feeling someone is actually going to take these ideas seriously and use them.)

Get Away With You

Dale Winton, Michelle McManus, Steve From *The X-Factor*, Jeanette Krankie, Keith Chegwin and Professor Susan Greenfield face the awesome task of becoming tour reps in Ibiza over Christmas and New Year. They must make sure all the holidaymakers get to their required destinations, that they imbibe copious amounts of alcohol and take part in ridiculous drinking games – or they face the wrath of Judith Chalmers. Hosted by Suzi 'permanently on holiday with a glass of wine in her hand' Perry.

Hell's Driving School

Vanessa Feltz, ex-*Blue Peter* star Stuart Miles, Sophie Aldred, Linda Robson, ex-Tory leader Michael Howard and Kenzie from Blazin' Squad have three months to train to become driving instructors. They must each get five celebrity pupils through their tests – to be shown live on Christmas Day on ITV opposite the Queen's Message. If they fail, they face the wrath of Jeremy Clarkson and Tiff Needell. Hosted by Kate Humble.

Celebrity Turkey Race

A crack team of would-be celeb chefs – Lady Isabella Whatsherface, Noooooooormski, Judy 'Can't Be With You Tonight' Boucher, Toby 'Can't get arrested' Anstis, Su '*Hi-De-Hi*' Pollard and Roger Black – all give up their Christmas Day to come and work in a Salvation Army hostel, cooking Christmas lunch for the armies of starving homeless under the tutelage of Delia 'Go on, my son!' Smith and Gordon 'fucking' Ramsay. The twist is that they all have to do it with one hand tied behind their backs, and that they can only communicate in sign language. Or something. I don't know.

God Gimme Strength

It's the busiest time of the year for our men and women of the cloth, and six luckless celebs are about to find out just how hot it can get in the vestry. Donning a dog collar for the whole of December will be Angela Rippon, Tim Vincent, Paris Hilton, Sean Maguire, Louise Nurding and Jeremy Beadle. The celebs will be living together in a purpose-built vicarage and will have weekly Bible study tasks, as well as sermons to prepare and deliver, parishioners to comfort and weddings, funerals and christenings to perform. As Christmas draws nearer and the pace gathers, who will be the first to crack under the strain of preparing a *Nine Lessons and Carols* service while chairing the Parish Christmas Fair Committee? Hosted by Carol Vorderman.

Celebrity Superstore

Possibly the cruellest one of all. Dani Behr, Dr Neil Fox, Magenta DeVine, MC Hammer, Fatima Whitbread and the Reverend Roger Royle are stripped of their trappings and forced to work shifts all through December in Poundland, Wilkinson's, Superdrug and TK Maxx, with the wearing of Santa hats compulsory. Celebs are marked out of ten for their rudeness, irritability and incompetence. Every week up to Christmas the viewers get to do a Superstore Stand-off, voting out their least favourite – they get to see the till-light of the chosen evictee flashing before they are led away. Each week, the length of the shift is ramped up and the celebs are, unknown to them, given decaf in place of their usual cup of coffee. Watch them slowly collapse.

And if it all gets too much for you, pop over to www.newgrounds.com/assassin to demonstrate what you really think of them all.

32

Yellow Snow and Other Hazards

Crisis at Christmas

Funnily enough, there may be times when it all goes wrong. Here is a helpful list of the most frequently occurring domestic crises at Christmas:

1. Heating Failure. Affected: 5.2m/11% of GB population
OK, so a white Christmas only exists in the fevered imagination of Bing Crosby these days, but there's no doubting that it's nearly always bollock-freezingly cold. So the prospect of having no heating over the festive period is not a pleasant one. If all else fails, you may find yourself chopping up the tree to put on the fire.

2. Electricity Failure/Power Cuts. Affected: 4.7m/10% of GB population
Aah, how romantic and seasonal it is to sing Christmas carols by candlelight. Well, not when that's all you've got.

3. Vehicle Breakdown. Affected: 4.3m/9% of GB population
Disappointingly, this may mean that you can't collect Auntie Gladys from the station.

4. Being Locked Out. Affected: 2.8m/6% of GB population
The most susceptible to this one are 16- to 24-year-olds, with 19% of them having experienced being left out in the cold at some point. Well, maybe it'll do them good.

5. Oven Failure. Affected: 2.8m/6% of GB population

Trying to cook the turkey on a gas hob is not fun. Perhaps a Turkey Madras from the local Indian is in order?

6. Burst Pipes. Affected: 2.4m/5% of GB population

You want those icicles on the outside of your house to look convincing, but not *that* convincing. Trying to get a plumber out on Christmas Eve can be fun. Ripping people off is obviously ingrained into their psyche. One imagines that, after the first caveman discovered he could carry water in animal-skin containers, it wasn't too long before Ugg's Plumbing was set up in the back room of his cave. Ugg would take a look at the holes in people's makeshift bottles, wince through his beard and make grunting noises which could be roughly translated as: 'Oooh, well, I can patch this for yer, guv, but this sort of rodent skin's hard to get hold of, you see, and the mammoth delivery doesn't arrive until next Thursday, so I'm afraid it's gonna cost yer.'

7. Television Broken. Affected: 2.4m/5% of GB population

Just think, you might get to miss the Queen's Message. Actually, has anyone got a hammer?...

8. Forgot to buy Alcohol. Affected: 1.9m/4% of GB population

Looks as if it's orange juice all round, then. It wouldn't do any harm for some sections of the populace to be deprived of alcohol, though. Think about it – you're woken at 2 a.m. on Christmas morning by screams and shouts of delight. No, it's not the children opening their presents – just a bunch of youths on their way back from an extended-hours drinking session. Obviously that's just what Christmas was made for. You lean out of the window and remonstrate with the yobs, but they retaliate with some interesting hand signals and a rude version of 'Good King Wenceslas' before vomiting on your flowerbeds. You slam the window shut and make a mental note to write to your MP about the compulsory electronic tagging of teenagers and the imposition of nationwide curfews. Again.

9. Phone Broken. Affected: 1.9m/4% of GB population
So you won't be phoning for that takeaway after all.

Yule Be Sorry
The Christmas period is fraught with danger – so much so that it's probably a good idea not to set foot outside your door during the whole of December. At least it would be, if it were not for the fact that most accidents happen in the home.

Those seasonal funsters the Royal Society for the Prevention of Accidents and those laugh-a-minute pranksters the TUC give annual advice to people attending office Christmas parties. This generally includes exhortations not to:

- Dance on tables, as you might fall off and injure yourself.

- Make reproductions of parts of your anatomy on the office photocopier, as the glass could break and cause injury to sensitive areas.

- Put up mistletoe, as it could encourage staff sexual harassment.

- Drink to excess.

It strikes me that this isn't really going far enough. They could always add to the list of proscribed activities, telling people that it's also inadvisable to:

- Eat mistletoe, given that it's poisonous – toxins in the berries can slow down the heart and cause hallucinations. (On the other hand, pagan druids would use it to break epileptic seizures and ward off witches – not at the same time, one presumes.)

🎄 Eat anything, in fact, given the number of party foods that are fattening, high in additives or might kill you.

🎄 Talk to anyone, as they might see this as unwanted sexual advances.

🎄 Give anyone a Christmas card, as they might be an atheist and would take this as a culturally inappropriate gesture.

🎄 Donate money to the office Christmas collection for the local hospice, as charity can be economically destabilising and fosters a culture of dependency.

🎄 Breathe, given the number of pollutants in the air (especially when Keith from Accounts has had a few).

33

Be Careful Out There

Here are some more thoughts about the kind of mishaps which might well befall you over the festive season. Take care now.

🎄 Just before Christmas 2004, Playtex, the makers of the **Wonderbra**, recalled their 'Deep Plunge Deeply Daring' model, designed for plunging necklines, when it was discovered that the strap could easily snap. (Presumably thousands of men then rushed out to buy one for their wives before they vanished from the shelves.)

🎄 'People think **fairy lights** last for ever – they don't, and can kill. They get crumpled and heaped into the attic for the rest of the year. Wires get bent, frayed and knotted and can all too easily lead to electrocution,' says RoSPA Safety Advisor David Jenkins. Apparently 12 per cent of Christmas injuries – mainly burns and electric shocks – are caused by fairy lights.

🎄 **Candles** are another source of danger. David Jenkins from RoSPA is back again: 'Candles are popular gifts at the moment, but they pose a major threat. They should never be left unattended or near anything that can catch fire, like curtains or decorations.' (Presumably Mr Jenkins added that you should also avoid sitting in the middle of the road during rush-hour, that it might be inadvisable to file your nails with a kitchen knife, and that it can be silly to stand on top of a hill during a storm brandishing a wet sword and shouting, 'Thunder-gods, do your worst!')

🎄 Meanwhile, 41 per cent of Christmas accidents are caused by people falling off chairs, tables and ladders while putting up **decorations**. These injuries could be reduced to zero by the simple act of not putting up decorations.

🎄 And then there are the specific dangers of **tinsel**. Chipping Sodbury school in Gloucestershire banned the wearing of tinsel on its non-uniform day in 2004 because of the health and safety dangers. Deputy headteacher Mel Jeffries said: 'We want our children to enjoy Christmas and have a good time, but at the same time making sure there are no accidents to spoil it. If tinsel is worn loosely around the neck it can be pulled tight and we don't want anything like that.' Let's hope nobody tried to throttle anyone with a deadly tie once they got back into uniform.

🎄 Don't forget **wrapping**. Ribbons and string can cause problems for cats. That's problems as in making them choke to death if they get hold of them.

🎄 Lighting the **Christmas pudding** can result in a nasty 'flashback' effect – no, nothing to do with suddenly remembering the awful thing which Uncle Frank said to Auntie Bethan over the sprouts in 1995. This is caused by people continuing to pour brandy on to the pudding once the match is lit.

🎄 **Trees** are responsible for approximately 34 per cent of Christmas accidents: those on offer include being poked in the eye by branches, back-strain from lifting the thing into the house, scratches from foliage and cuts caused by inexpert attempts at pruning. It sounds like the stuff of a bad sci-fi novel, but 2,000 people a year are attacked by their Christmas trees.

And while we're at it, let's mention some odd stuff called 'Prolong', which you can spray on your pine tree to stop it shedding. Or maybe you'd better not. If you ingest the stuff, a safety campaign warns, it can cause diarrhoea and vomiting. (One sometimes has to wonder who these safety campaigns are aimed at. You do know you're not supposed to drink bleach either, right? And that jumping off tall buildings is dangerous?)

While we're on the subject of **foliage** – the Christmas cherry is a popular houseplant, but its unripened orange berries can cause stomach pains. The Christmas rose, sometimes called the snow rose or winter rose, is toxic if eaten in large quantities – apparently it's such an effective cause of diarrhoea that it was used as a purgative by the ancient Greeks. The seer Melampus used the plant to cure the madness of King Proteus' daughters, who had become convinced that they were cows.

Taking a heavy **turkey** out of the oven can cause a condition known as 'turkey-lifter's back'. Presumably one is meant to observe the technique of Russian weightlifters at the Olympics before attempting such a feat.

Alcohol is the most common source of Christmas ailments and injuries. It's plentiful at Christmas, of course, and everybody gets in far more than they need. There will always be the assumption that people want to sample stuff which they wouldn't touch with a bargepole at any other time of the year, such as Harvey's Bristol Cream or Kahlúa, and this will lead to swift inebriation and some unfortunate incidents. The festive tipple is responsible for everything from punch-ups at the office party to aggravating depression and bringing about surprise pregnancies. (On the other hand, wasn't it one of the latter which started the whole Christmas thing off?)

The party season can sometimes cause **deafness**, warns the Royal National Institute for the Deaf. (I said, 'THE PARTY SEASON CAN SOMETIMES…' Ahem.) Dance floor noise can reach 110 decibels, which is the equivalent of the levels produced by a jet engine. The RNID advice for those going out to clubs and gigs over the festive season is to stand well away from the speakers, take regular breaks and consider wearing earplugs. (This is especially advisable if you're thinking of attending a Mariah Carey concert.)

And don't forget the danger of being blinded by houses bedecked with dazzling Stars of Bethlehem and streams of 'icicle-effect' lights – or of your children being scared to death by evil, dark-eyed fibreglass Santas flashing on and off.

34

Is It Me?

Yes, it seems that the Great British Public has quite an impressive record when it comes to self-inflicted harm over the festive season. Here are a few statistics about the average number of British people who die each year in the following inventive ways:

● Eating glass Christmas baubles in the belief that they were chocolate: 19 people

● Testing a 9-volt battery on their tongue: 3 people

● Watering the Christmas tree while the lights were plugged in: 31 people

It beggars belief – and it does make you wonder if anybody has died at Christmas by sticking a wet finger into a plug socket to see if it really would electrocute them, or jumping off the roof of the house to see how high it was.

As if that were not enough, many more are injured annually. In increasing order of casualty-count, the top injuries are:

● Broken arm from pulling a cracker: 4 people

● Injuries from Scalextric cars: 5 people

● Cracking skull while vomiting into toilet: 8 people

- ● Burns caused by trying on a new jumper with lit cigarette in mouth: 18 people

- ● Cuts caused by using a knife instead of a corkscrew: 58 people

- ● Injuries sustained by not taking all pins out of a new shirt before trying it on: 142 people

- ● Breaking teeth while attempting to open bottle of beer in mouth: 543 people

But – again according to RoSPA – the most dangerous Christmas presents ever are...well, have a guess. Electrical items, you might think? Indeed, there are about 200 accidents caused by electrical equipment each year, but they are by no means top of the Christmas tree. The runner-up categories were:

- ● No. 3: Tripping over wires from games consoles.

- ● No. 2: Choking incidents caused by coins in Christmas puddings.

So, what's top of the RoSPA pops? Is it stabbing by vicious toy gladiator swords, or horrible injuries caused by testing power tools on icy paths?

No – it's slippers. That's right, slippers. More people are admitted to hospital at Christmas following slipper-related incidents than at any other time of the year. It seems that those innocuous-looking items can be a major hazard, causing unwary people to lose their footing and pitch downstairs.

So, do Dad a favour, leave the novelty footwear alone and buy him a subscription to a Dangerous Sports club. In the long term, he'll be safer.

And finally...
A display outside Cheadle Hulme fire station – intended as a reminder about driving safely – featured a crashed car with Santa's legs protruding from the shattered windscreen. Firefighters were forced to remove the display after complaints from residents. 'It was a light-hearted gesture intended to portray a serious message,' said a spokesman, 'but some people haven't taken it in the right context.' One local woman who was disappointed to see the display taken down said, rather entertainingly, 'I think it's a good thing when people try to get over the seriousness of Christmas accidents.' Well, quite.

35

'Tis the Season To Be Stupid

Westminster council recently advised Londoners to look out for the following 'top scams' over the festive season. Some of them make you wonder if they expect the average Londoner to have a brain cell to rub together between them.

- Fake designer clothes (here's a clue: if you find a Versace dress for £15 in your local Cheapo, it's *probably* a fake, wouldn't you say?).

- Fake cosmetics and perfumes for sale (ditto as above, for Estée Lauder and Calvin Klein).

- Dodgy Christmas tree lights (if you buy them off a bloke in the market, you only have yourself to blame).

- Unsafe children's toys (ditto – if you want cheap ones, don't go to the market, trawl the charity shops and supermarket offers).

- Counterfeit vodka.

- Mobile phone text scams (if you can't spot one of these, you're not grown-up enough to have a mobile phone).

- Hotels double-booking your room (so stand your ground and complain – they're in the wrong, aren't they?).

🎄 Restaurant rip-offs at your office parties (you could always ask around other offices for reputable deals).

🎄 Overpriced theatre tickets (this is just a problem at Christmas, is it?).

🎄 Lottery scams based in Canada (easily solved – don't do the bloody lottery).

🎄 Candles causing a fire hazard (just a thought, but are you sure you're safe to be let out of the house?).

🎄 Dodgy plumbers fixing your frozen pipes (companies do advertise in the Yellow Pages, you know – they don't all come to your door touting for trade).

For some reason, they failed to mention a few others which might have sprung to mind, such as:

🎄 Fat, bearded men inviting your children to sit on their knee.

🎄 Extended episodes of drama series with 'winter' scenes filmed in bright sunlight, with all the trees in full leaf and characters clocking off for the evening when it's still light (hello, *Casualty*!). Do they think viewers are stu… Oh, OK.

🎄 Chocolate tree decorations in gaudy foil wrappers depicting children's TV characters, which, once unwrapped, have nothing to do with said characters apart from said discarded wrapping.

🎄 Free compilations of Christmas 'hits' which turn out to have cut vital corners in the production, such as: 'A Winter's Tale' by Michael Ball instead of the David Essex original, synth versions of 'When a Child is Born' performed by Keff

McCulloch with additional drum rolls and dramatic swoops and stabs, a pan pipes rendition of 'Saviour's Day' and an upbeat medley of well-known carols arranged by the Portsmouth Sinfonia and sung by Russell Watson with The Krankies, and Keith Harris and Orville.

Not to mention these rather particular seasonal difficulties which we hope no longer arise:

- Being ordered back to the place where you were born in order to be counted or 'taxed' (not even New Labour have tried that one yet, but maybe it's only a matter of time).

- Your girlfriend getting up the duff when you've not even slept together, and her trying to talk her way out of it by claiming it was some kind of spirit (yes, probably Kahlúa, love).

- Dishonest innkeepers charging you a fortune to sleep in a cowshed.

- Gentlemen from the East (of dubious sagacity) offering dodgy gifts.

36

Season of Goodwill?

Sometimes, the Christmas season just brings out the worst in people, as the following examples will illustrate.

🧦 A survey by the **British Cleaning Council** has found that two-thirds of office cleaners are never invited to the office Christmas party. One cleaner had worked for a company for eight years before she finally received an invitation to a work function, and was so angry that the offer had taken so long that she turned it down. So, if you come back to work on 2nd January to find your bin still full of old sausage rolls and wine bottles, you'll know who's annoyed with you and why.

🧦 Cardinal Cormac Murphy-O'Connor, leader of the Catholic Church in England and Wales, had a few words to say in 2004 about the way **Christian symbols** are denigrated over the Christmas period. He took particular issue with David and Victoria Beckham appearing as Joseph and Mary in a waxwork rendition of the Nativity, and an advertisement for the TV show *Shameless* using a parody of The Last Supper. 'It seems incredible that Christianity, particularly at Christmas, is displayed in a way that is so tasteless,' said the Cardinal. 'To have a very special part of Christianity depicted in this way and its most precious symbol, which is the coming of God into the world in Jesus Christ, seems to me to be not just disrespectful to Christians – it is also disrespectful to the heritage of Britain and also does damage to the culture of this country.' Quite true – after all, the last time anybody prayed before an image of David Beckham was when he took that penalty against Portugal, and look where that got us.

> **City councils** are no slackers when it comes to making a bit of money out of Christmas shoppers – one only has to look at what happened in Manchester in recent years. The cost of on-street parking in the city rose by 25 per cent at Christmas 2002 – and the free on-street parking on Saturday afternoons for which the city was renowned came to a sudden end. Of course, there was nothing to stop people driving out to the Trafford Centre, where parking remained free. And so now Manchester might end up seeing the same exodus from its city-centre shops that has already partly blighted Sheffield. Councillor Val Stevens, executive member for planning and transport said: 'These increases apply to only a small proportion, just 4 per cent, of the overall parking provision in the city centre. They are endorsed by the Chamber of Commerce and City Centre Management Company. The charges have remained static for several years and are now in line with other cities.' She also added 'Bah humbug.' Not really.

> The removal of a **statue of St Nicholas** in the Turkish province of Antalya didn't go down very well at all with some of the local residents – especially as it was replaced by a terribly tasteful plastic Santa Claus. The local mayor made a complaint to the Turkish president. St Nicholas's connections with the area are well documented – he lived in the local town of Demre in the fourth century.

> Funny how most people in this country, even those who profess to hate the Tory party, exhibit pure Conservative values of individualism and materialism and would never do anything collectivist without asking 'What's in it for me?' So this Christmas, instead of buying six Lotto tickets to

supplement your usual three, why not give six quid straight to whichever cause you ostensibly like to support? It would be a start. Because the Prole Tax is an insult to our national psyche. What is so insidiously offensive about it (apart from the fact that it spawns quiz shows hosted by Dale Winton and Julian Clary) is the way a money making venture dresses itself up as a provider for 'worthy causes' when it actually perpetuates and entrenches social exclusion. Communities are then expected to be pitifully grateful for the £30,000 contribution to a new hall (probably destined to be vandalised, graffitied and/or torched), whereas if they had all put their pound a week into a grass-roots fund, they might have been able to buy the thing themselves and actually draw some civic pride from it. But no, we are happy with the dependency culture.

A very PC Christmas

Also, the season always sees an increase in technological nastiness – fraud, spam, 'phishing' and the general spread of viruses. Unless you are one of these terribly clever people who can tweak the source for their own kernels (whatever the hell that means) and know exactly what goes on under the bonnet of their computer, then be especially careful on your last day in the office before the break.

And that applies afterwards too – if you get back from the holiday to find your inbox cluttered with more than the usual rubbish, you may not apply your normal standards of care and caution in dealing with it. You may have 400 messages awaiting you. OK, you may be happy to delete 395 of them, given that you haven't entered any international lotteries, you are reasonably happy with the size of your penis, you're not desperately bothered about Eastern European prostitutes with large breasts and you'd rather not assist any Nigerian banks in the transfer of funds. However, the 396th may well be that deadly attachment which claims to be a New Year greeting from Auntie Gladys. In reality, it's concealing a complex piece of code devised by some spotty 15-year-old from Utah who can't get a girlfriend and has filled in the time in between masturbating, listening to Slipknot and playing Doom by devising ever more horrid ways to fuck up your files. (It's a kind of virtual version of charging into the school library stripped to the waist, painted with mud and brandishing a machine gun.)

Generally, if it looks too good to be true, it probably is. It's amazing how people will fall for scams online when they never would do so in real life. You never see notes going round like this: 'BE CAREFUL! A bloke in a dirty mac with a clipboard has been turning up on doorsteps and saying he is conducting research into goosebumps. He will ask you to take off all your clothes and dance a jig for him on your front porch. THIS IS A SCAM! All he wants is to see you getting naked. Send this message to everyone you know!'

What's Another Year?

t's over. So how do you feel? Uplifted, fulfilled, at one with Nature, your body's natural harmony restored? Or fraught, frazzled and frustrated, thanking all your lucky stars and assorted deities that you won't have to go through that for another year?

If it's the latter, then welcome to the club.

A well-known 'lifestyle guru' has written about the ways in which you can immediately assess what went wrong this year and how you can immediately make plans for next Christmas in order to learn from your mistakes. Hmm. Let's have a look at a few of her suggestions, shall we?

1 'Did your Christmas menus work out well? Did you have something to offer an unexpected vegetarian guest?'

Oh, yes, I'm going to get a sodding nut roast in specially next year, and cook that special separate pudding with no animal fat in it. Am I bollocks. Any vegetarians turning up 'unexpectedly' at my house on Christmas Day are perfectly welcome to eat the leftover vegetables.

2 'What did you have for the children who wouldn't eat vegetables?'

I'll tell you what I had for them. A special treat called 'being sent to your room without any pudding', familiar to children down the ages.

3 'Did you forget to warm the plates or chill the wine?'

Do you know, with everything else that was going on it must have slipped my mind. I wondered what the plates were doing in the fridge, and who'd inadvertently sneaked that bottle of Chablis into the oven.

4 'When it's time to take down the cards, take a few minutes to make a Christmas card list in the back of your new diary or address book. This will make writing out your cards easier next year as you won't be worried about forgetting anyone.'

And I should be bothered about this *why*, exactly? Anyone who takes offence at not getting a card from me can take a running jump.

5 'Take a good look at your tree and room decorations. Are some of them looking past their best? Would you love to start again with a new theme or colour scheme or add just a few new items to give the whole look a lift?'

Yes, that's just what I'm going to do. I'm going to replace my entire collection of Christmas decorations to fit in with a 'new colour scheme' so that in two years' time some overpaid, ponytailed twonk can tell me that, darling, silver is *soooo* mid-decade, you really ought to be going with red and gold.

6 'Did a friend's decorating scheme inspire you or did you see a wonderful decorating idea in a department store or craft shop?'

Yes, I was so inspired by the people up the road with their 6-foot-high neon Mary and Joseph, their inflatable Rudolph and their 200 feet of flashing icicles that I'm going to rush out and buy myself exactly the same thing for next year. I'm sorry, what kind of life do you imagine I have?

7 'Don't forget to stock up on clear or coloured cellophane and tissue paper to wrap all those gifts or gift baskets that you intend to make yourself.'

Thanks, I might have forgotten about that. As you know, I like nothing better in the December evenings than sitting down with my craft box full of cellophane and rustling up a few *Blue Peter*-style presents for all the family. Tell you what, why don't I hand-make all my cards myself from glitter, buttons and old cereal boxes? Even better, I could cobble together a tree from Leyland Cypress offcuts and decorate it with cunningly fashioned foil animals. You see, the thing is, I just have too much time on my hands.

8 'Now is the time to hit the sales for cards, decorations and wrapping paper, as all these items can be found at half their usual price or less.'

Oh, for God's sake, do you *have* a life? And if you think I'm going anywhere near the January sales you are seriously deluded.

9 'Treat yourself to a couple of crates or storage boxes to pack away your decorations neatly and label them so that they are easy to find.'

I've got a better idea. Shove the decorations in an old cardboard box and put it in the cellar. Then treat yourself to a large whisky and put your feet up.

10 'Resolve to spread the financial load next year by making a list of everyone that you want to give gifts to and make or buy one or two each month throughout the year.'

Or resolve to spread the financial load next year by simply cutting people off your Christmas list. It's cheaper and quicker.

11 'Spend a few minutes to think about what gave you pleasure this Christmas. Who did you really enjoy spending time with? Who did you hate spending time with? Would you have enjoyed something a little more spiritual? Make a note to attend a midnight mass or a carol service or get yourself an invite to the local nativity play.'

You were actually doing quite well there until the bit about getting more spiritual.

12 'It will only take a few minutes to note down these things now, yet once you are back into your regular routines they are easily forgotten.'

Yes, they are, and thank God for that. Why on earth would I want to be reminded of them before next year?

38

Christmas By Numbers

£50 Estimated minimum expenditure needed to decorate a house with 'icicle' effect lights.

1.2 million Number of bulbs annually displayed on exterior of house owned by Danny and Anne Meikle of Coalburn, Lanarkshire.

£4000 – 5000 Electricity bill for Christmas period expected by Danny and Anne Meikle of Coalburn, Lanarkshire.

12 Number of party balloons which could be filled by the carbon dioxide generated from a normal string of Christmas tree lights used for 10 hours a day for 12 days.

£20,000 Amount for charity raised in six years by John Hutchinson of County Tyrone by turning his house into Santa's Grotto.

1 Chart placing of Bob The Builder's single 'Can We Fix It' at Christmas 2000.

2 Chart placing of Eminem's single 'Stan' at Christmas 2000.

3 Number of UK Christmas number-one singles by the Spice Girls ('2 Become 1', 1996; 'Too Much', 1997; 'Goodbye', 1998).

3 Number of UK Christmas number-one singles by Cliff Richard ('I Love You', 1960; 'Mistletoe And Wine', 1988; 'Saviour's Day', 1990). 'The Millennium Prayer' in 1999 was knocked off the top at Christmas by Westlife.

9 Number of times Slade's 'Merry Xmas Everybody' was in the charts between 1973 and 1998 (including a 1980 re-recording with the Reading Choir and a 1998 remix by Flush).

11 Number of oaks in UK on which mistletoe grows.

13% Percentage of men who 'actively enjoy' shopping. (And we reckon half of them were lying while the rest were talking about CDs and books.)

6 Number of Marks & Spencer stores in UK which were equipped in 2004 with 'crèches for men', featuring sofas, TVs, Scalextric sets and remote-controlled bikes.

80,000 Estimated number of people in the UK who end up in hospital over the Christmas period.

4 Number of broken arms reported in UK in 2003 as a result of 'cracker-pulling incidents'.

142 Number of people in UK injured in 1999 as a result of not removing all the pins from new shirts.

24% Percentage of children questioned in a survey who said they would like Father Christmas to bring them a computer.

8% Percentage of parents in same survey planning to buy their children a computer.

25% Percentage of children questioned in a survey who said they would like Father Christmas to bring them an iPod.

9% Percentage of parents in same survey planning to buy their children an iPod.

17% Seasonally unadjusted sales growth in December 2004 – the lowest level since records began in 1961.

£26.47 Average price of a Christmas present in 2004.

40% Proportion of presents bought in the two weeks before Christmas Day.

85% Percentage of people surveyed by the website shopping. com intending to use the Internet to do most of their Christmas shopping.

$1700 Top bid on eBay received by a 41-year-old Pasadena father who put his 11- and 14-year-old children's Christmas presents up for auction on the website as a punishment for the boys' bad behaviour. The money was donated to their local church.

4% Likelihood that, some time in the next decade, the Queen's Christmas Message will be followed by an interactive phone vote asking whether she should abdicate.

1% Likelihood of Queen's Christmas Message ever being done by Duchess of Cornwall (formerly Mrs Camilla Parker Bowles).

39

The Christmas Checklist

We are coming to the end of our dissection of all that is worst about the Christmas period. It's quite telling that when you get back to work and ask, 'What was your Christmas like, then?' you don't see people's eyes light up. They don't jump up and down and begin exclaiming that it was the most wonderful time of year, that they loved seeing their family and unwrapping all their presents, that Christmas Day was fabulous and they can't wait to do it all over again in twelve months. No, they say, 'Oh, it was all right,' or, 'Oh, it was quiet.' And you can feel vindicated.

Here's a little game for you to finish with – in the hope that it will help you remain sane throughout the weeks of madness.

> 🎄 Shell-suited slapper with snotty kids, buying handfuls of extra lottery tickets: 1 point. 2 points if she physically assaults the offspring while in the queue. 3 points if staff have to manhandle her. 4 points for a full fight.
>
> 🎄 Shop staff in 'amusing' Santa hats: 1 point. With springs of holly: 2 points. With holly and tinsel: 3 points.
>
> 🎄 1 point for local lights switched on by D-list celebrity. 2 points if D-lister has appeared on a 'reality' TV show. 3 points if this is how they became 'famous' in the first place. 4 points if someone in the audience asks 'who's he/she?'

Cadbury's Creme Eggs already on display: 1 point. Actually being bought: 2 points.

Clergyman sounding off in media about 'true meaning of Christmas'. An extra point if it's the Archbishop of Canterbury.

Invitation to party from someone you don't know: 1 point. Invitation to party from someone you don't like: 2 points.

Card from someone you don't know: 1 point. Card from someone you don't like: 2 points. Card from a company from whom you ordered something on the Internet in 1999: 3 points.

Christmas circular: 1 point. A bonus point if it's from someone you haven't seen for over 15 years.

'Battle' for this year's Christmas number one is announced: 1 point. Bonus point if the front runner is a children's TV character or someone from a *Pop Idol/Popstars*-type programme.

First glowing Santa appears on porch roof somewhere on your street: 1 point. Even bigger glowing Santa appears further down your street: 2 points.

Children announce desire for presents vastly outside your price range: 1 point. Children told that they are lucky to get anything because there are kids starving in Africa and told not to be so bloody ungrateful: 2 points. Give yourself 5 whole extra points if you actually play them the bit from the *Live Aid* video with the starving Ethiopians.

40

The Ballad of the Modern-Day Scrooge

This year, I'm not bothering with Christmas,
Or peace and goodwill to all men.
You can all call me names, but I'm not playing games
Of charades by the fireside again.

I don't want to buy Christmas bargains,
To wrap and stack under the tree,
The socks and the books, the daft TV cooks
Are unbearably maudlin and twee.

This year, I'm not shopping at Christmas,
Or buying your family a present.
It's not that I'm mean, but your lights are obscene
And your children are deeply unpleasant.

I don't want to hear Christmas music,
Bing Crosby and Cliff and Greg Lake,
And East 17, Michael Bublé and Queen
Can chuck themselves out with the cake.

I don't want to hear Christmas carols
Of heralds and angels and kings,
Your snowmen and holly are so far from jolly
They make me think murderous things.

This year, I'm not eating at Christmas,
I don't want a lunch with four courses,
And I'm not really keen on watching the Queen
And repeats of last year's *Fools And Horses*.

This year, I'm not bothering with Christmas,
So don't wish me a *Joyeux Noël*;
Your seasonal greetings are meaningless bleatings,
And your jumper is awful as well.

This year, I'm not bothering with Christmas,
It's the sensible thing – I'm not bitter.
All those baubles and lights take all day to get right,
And your floor gets all covered with glitter.

This year, I'm not bothering with Christmas,
The turkey can stay there unplucked,
There'll be no Secret Santa or family banter,
And 'joy to the world' can get knotted.